CPR from Combat

CPR from Combat

ISBN 13: 979-8-218-91264-2
Library of Congress Control Number: 2026900712

Edited by Elizabeth Boerner
Layout and Cover Design by Helen Ounjian

This work depicts actual events of the author, recalled and recorded as truthfully as permitted to remain consistent with the recollection. Dialogue may be embellished but within the nature of the character depicted. Names of characters have been changed to respect their privacy.

Scripture quotations taken from The Holy Bible, New International Version®, NIV®. Copyright © 1973, 1978, 1984, 2011 by Biblica, Inc. Used with permission of Zondervan. All rights reserved worldwide. www.zondervan.com. Scripture quotations marked (NLT) are taken from the Holy Bible, New Living Translation, copyright © 1996, 2004, 2015 by Tyndale House Foundation. Used by permission of Tyndale House Publishers, Carol Stream, Illinois 60188, USA. All rights reserved. Scripture taken from the New King James Version®. Copyright © 1982 by Thomas Nelson. Used by permission. All rights reserved. Scripture quotations are from the ESV® Bible (The Holy Bible, English Standard Version®), © 2001 by Crossway, a publishing ministry of Good News Publishers. ESV Text Edition: 2025. The ESV text may not be quoted in any publication made available to the public by a Creative Commons license. The ESV may not be translated in whole or in part into any other language. Used by permission. All rights reserved. Scripture quotations taken from the (NASB®) New American Standard Bible®, Copyright © 1960, 1971, 1977, 1995, 2020 by The Lockman Foundation. Used by permission. All rights reserved. www.Lockman.org. Scripture quotations taken from the Amplified® Bible (AMP), Copyright © 2015 by The Lockman Foundation. Used by permission. www. Lockman.org

Perfect Misfits LLC
An Independent Publishing Company
For inquiries, contact perfectmisfits.de@gmail.com

Printed in the United States of America

Perfect Misfits LLC
An Independent Publishing Company

CPR FROM COMBAT

CHRIST'S PEACE RESTORATION FROM COMBAT

Dismantling the Sandbag Fortress Around My Heart

Tony Funtanilla

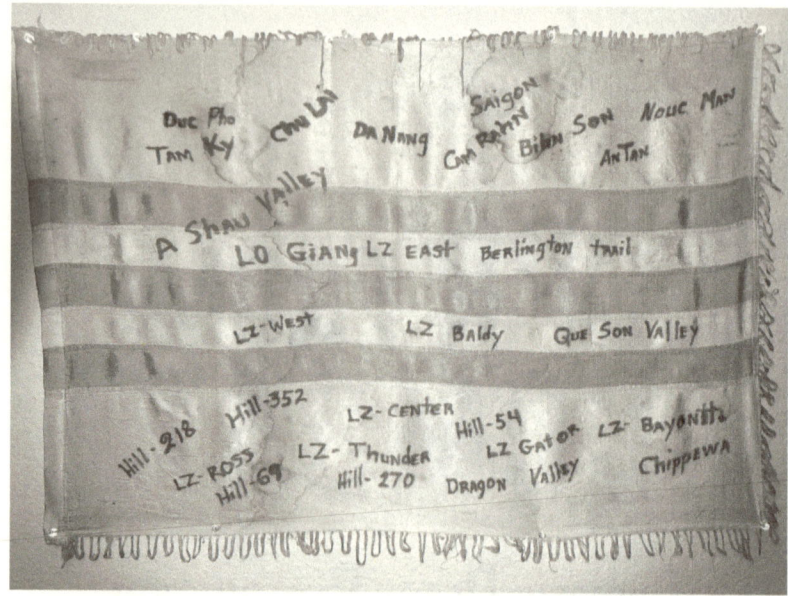

I grabbed this flag from a bombed-out schoolhouse as a souvenir before heading home. This flag was the former national flag of South Vietnam before North Vietnam took it over, and after we withdrew at the end of our involvement in the war.

Once home, I wrote the names of places where some of my most memorable battles took place. It is irreplaceable and invaluable to me because it is a tangible representation of the past from which God has healed me, and it can now be used to help others.

MY DEEPEST APPRECIATION TO...

First and foremost, I thank God for graciously providing me with the encouragement, inspiration, and revelations to write about my journey. I thank God for adding His useful purpose to my traumatic past.

Thank you, God, also, for blessing me with my wife Debbie, who never gave up on me, always encouraged me, always prayed for me, always knew how to talk me back from the jungle, and loved me exactly the way God knew I needed to be loved.

And thank you Lord for the many spiritually influential people You have set in place along my life's path who have spoken Your truth, love, enlightenment, and so much encouragement into my life; Pastor Jaime Pierce; All of the Pastoral Staff at HighRidge Church; My brothers in Christ from the Gate Keepers Ministry, especially Paul Rider and George Patton; My dear fellow worship warriors, Gerry and Gayle McKnight; and finally to my publisher Elizabeth Boerner for championing me with her prayers and faith in this writing endeavor.

I would also like to steal this opportunity to publicly apologize to the people I hurt or offended during my earlier years of emotional absence and character dysfunction; to my daughters and grandchildren; and to all of my past friends and relationships. God willing, I hope someday to have the chance to express my deep apologies in person.

Psalm 13 (NIV)

How long, Lord? Will you forget me forever?
How long will You hide Your face from me?
How long must I wrestle with my thoughts **(flash-backs)**
and day after day have sorrow **(regret, discontentment,**
anguish)
in my heart?

How long will my enemy **(the Viet Cong)**
triumph over me?
Look on me and answer, Lord my God.
Give light to my eyes,
or I will sleep in death **(from constant nightmares)**,
and my enemy **(Post Traumatic Stress)**
will say, "I have overcome him,"
and my foes **(the Viet Cong)** *will rejoice when I fall.*

But I trust in Your unfailing love;
my heart rejoices in Your salvation **(my healing)**.
I will sing the Lord's praise,
for He has been good to me
(He restored my "heart peace").

PREFACE

You can take a soldier out of the war, but you can't take the war out of the soldier. However, I am now living proof that my God is stronger than PTSD. My loving God has graciously removed its sting so that my past no longer dictates my inability to feel, love, and trust to any healthy depth. I still wear the scars, but that's all they are; they are no longer open wounds that are inflamed, infectious, or painful. I now wear them with gratitude as a testament of the past that God has delivered me from.

Genesis 50:20 (NLT)

You intended to harm me, but God intended it all for good. He brought me to this position so I could save the lives of many people.

I have not intended for this book to be any sort of devotional or "how-to self-help" magic bullet. I only felt compelled to share my story of victory over my emotional trauma from my war experiences. I can only credit my transformation to my reliance on God. I am fully convinced of this belief because I am living proof of all that I have experienced on the following pages: the bad, the ugly, and then the good. Those closest to me, especially my fantastic wife of over 44 years, can attest firsthand to my "before and after." My hope and prayer is that my open honesty will encourage others who also struggle with the torment of PTSD to just consider what has brought me peace and healing, and perhaps just give it a try. Not just for Combat Veterans, but First Responders and anyone who feels emotionally shackled from traumatic life events.

I am fully convinced that PTSD is a tactic used by a spiritual enemy who tries to keep us down, distracted, and disoriented. But God desires to deliver us from our traumatic fog so that others can find peace and hope through the credibility of our testimonies. We only have to trust God with our "yes" and to give Him all of the glory, so that our past no longer hinders us from being the fruitful influencers He created us to be. Some of you may not believe in this kind of thing and think that Christians only rely on this "God thing" as a crutch rather than a lifeboat. The truth is, one of us is right and one of us is wrong. My question is simply: who stands to lose the most if they are wrong?

Some of my accounts in this book may be disturbingly graphic, but I've included them so that you might better understand and respect why many combat veterans choose not to talk about our war experiences. In order to talk about the details, we must *remember them*. To remember them, *we're forced to relive them*. When reliving them, the memories have been so embedded down deep in our subconscious that they begin to look, feel, taste, and smell far too vivid all over again. Memories of the things we witnessed, did, should or should not have done are painful evidence that we lived out the worst and most barbaric that a human being could be.

Also, in some of these passages, I have chosen not to use full or real names out of respect for the dignity of family members who might read this book.

Glossary

60	M-60 Machine gun
15:30 Hours	Military time for 3:30 PM
Agent Orange	Defoliant Chemical used to kill large areas of vegetation
Arty	Artillery Fire
AWOL	Absent Without Leave (Unauthorized absence)
C- Rations	WWII box of canned food and sundries
Charlie	Viet Cong, VC, Victor Charles
Civies	Civilian cloths
Cobra	Gunship helicopter Armed with rockets and mini-Gatling guns
Contact	(see Fire Fight)
Cordite	Substance used in gun powder or explosive devices
CP	Command Post or position
Dink	Derogatory slang for Vietnamese person
Duce and a half	2½ ton military truck
Fire Fight	Any hostile engagement with the enemy
Friendlies	Comrades, non-enemies
GI	American soldier
Gook	Derogatory slang for Vietnamese person
Humping the Bush	Patrolling on missions anywhere outside of a friendly/secure base
In Country	Vietnam
Jerry can	5.3 gallon metal can used to store water or fuel
Klicks	Kilometers
LST	Heavy equipment transportation Navy ship
Mermite Can	Large insulated metal container used to keep food warm
NVA	North Vietnamese Army, well trained and equipped enemy soldiers
O.A.B.	Oakland Army Base
Poncho	wearable plastic rain tarp
Recon	Reconnaissance, observe, or investigate
Sit Rep	Situation Report, What's going on, What is the current situation?
The Bush	Any place out in a field of operation, outside of the wire
The World	America, USA, Home
VC	Viet Cong, Victor Charles

INNOCENT ADOLESCENCE

MY "LEAVE IT TO BEAVER" CHILDHOOD

Over the years, I've heard many people tell about their childhoods being severely impacted by various forms of drama or trauma. Some are impacted by divorce, others by abuse, or substance addictions, immoral or even criminal behavior, death or catastrophic illness, or parental absenteeism. Mine, however, seemed so boring and uneventful in comparison. I grew up in a home with both parents and one older brother. The only yelling and screaming in anger or hostility that I can recall ever hearing came from my dad watching wrestling, Oakland A's, or Raiders ball games on TV.

At least once per month, we would always have some form of family gathering with all of my aunts, uncles, cousins, and maternal grandparents in attendance, typical of most Filipino families. Every adult friend of the family was addressed by all of us children as "Uncle" or "Auntie," which gave them all the love and respect due a blood relative. This even included the authority to discipline us if necessary. There was always an abundance of food, singing, laughter, games, and love.

Oddly, the most traumatic event that I can recall growing up was when my dad broke his leg. He fell off a garbage can while jumping up and down on the overflowing trash to smash it all down. Thankfully, though, it sounds so mundane compared to many other family stories I've listened to over the years.

My father was the eldest of 6 siblings and left the Philippines at the tender age of 16 in search of a more promising life here in America. When WWII broke out, he joined the Navy to fight for this country that he came to love so much. The motivation to fight was magnified when he learned that the Japanese invaded the Philippines and forced one of his younger brothers, "Tony," to dig his own grave. Tony was then brutally executed. I later took on that uncle's namesake to honor my father's side of our family. When the war ended, my father was granted automatic US citizenship as America's way of thanking him for honorably serving in the military.

My father only had an eighth-grade education, so his best option to provide for his budding family was to become a Life Insurance Salesman. By day, he managed his client's accounts. By night, he networked with potential insurance customers by joining organizations such as the American Legion, the Knights of Columbus, and the VFW. We weren't rich by any means, but we always had a roof over our heads, two cars in the garage, food on the table, and clothes on our backs. I was too young to understand why my father wasn't available to teach me things like how to play ball, go camping, or fish with the fathers of my neighborhood friends. I envied them and often wished I had a father more like theirs. It wasn't until he retired and I had a family of my own to support that I truly understood his hard work and absence were driven by his honorable character and deep love for us.

Whenever my brother and I needed to be disciplined, Dad would sit us both down and make us tell him why we thought the infraction was wrong. If there was any way to fix or avoid repeating it, then spanked us. As I recall, he never spanked us out of anger or with excessive force. It always stung, but we understood why it needed to. No matter who committed the naughty deed, we both always faced the punishment. He would punish the one who committed the infraction, and the other one of us for not talking the guilty one out of doing it in the first place. In theory, it was a smart concept, but in reality, being just kids, we'd always end up doing whatever we wanted anyway. At the time, the reward of possibly getting away with the no-nos always blinded me to the consequences.

My mother was born in the Hawaiian Islands. She was the third oldest of seven siblings. When my mother was 3years old, they moved to the Central California area, where she grew up and eventually met and married my father while he was home on leave after the war. Mom was always the go-to person when every my brother or I needed coddling or a sympathetic ear. The only seemingly emotionally abusive thing that ever came out of her mouth was probably, "Wait till your father gets home." I chuckle to myself now at how *dreadful* it is for a child to have to worry about it all day long. During my childhood and until her retirement, she also worked. She was employed at the Oakland Army Base in Oakland, California, as a clerk typist. It wasn't until after I returned home from the Army that she told me what her job entailed.

Mom's job was to process manifests listing the names of the bodies returning home from Vietnam who were killed in action.

My mother worked with Betty, who was her closest friend and coworker. One day, my mother saw that Betty's son's name appeared on the list. Mom toiled in anguish with a broken heart, trying to decide if she should tell Betty about the discovery and risk punitive repercussions for a breach of her employer's security protocol. If she chose to keep the find to herself, Betty would know my mother would have known—what then? My mother wisely decided to consult her supervisor, and together they approached her soon-to-be devastated friend.

-♦-

My brother fought in Vietnam for 18 months, immediately followed by my 12-month tour there. This meant that for nearly 3 years, every day, poor mom would hold her breath and desperately pray against the horror of possibly discovering her son's name on one of those manifests. It's no wonder that she suffered from stress-related ulcers.

-♦-

In February of 1968, while in Vietnam, I received word that my mother was in the hospital because her ulcers had ruptured and was in serious condition, in need of immediate surgery. I tried desperately to be granted emergency leave to go home. However, at that time, all of South Vietnam was in the middle of the extreme chaos caused by the Tet Offensive. As a result, there was a growing need to replace lost ground-level leadership due to casualty attrition. At the relatively young age of 19, I was quickly promoted to Sergeant and assigned a squad of eight other lives to lead. Emergency leave request ….DENIED!

So there I was, 19 years old, stuck in Vietnam, having to organize, motivate, and give orders to 8 other 18 to 20-year-olds to do very dangerous things that could get them killed or wounded.

In retrospect, all these memories are representative of how very loving and protective my family was. I now have a better understanding of the price families also pay to support their loved ones' service to our country.

My point is that sometimes we can become so near-sighted and self-absorbed with our own choices and desires that we fail to consider that other people may be experiencing similar or far worse challenges. More regrettably, how fallout from our own well-intended actions or choices can drastically impact the lives of those around us, especially our loved ones. With deep regret, I wish to God that I could have the chance to apologize to my Mom and Dad for what I put them through. Unfortunately, they have both been gone from this life for several years now. I strongly suggest to you that if you have apologies to make, do it now while you have the chance, rather than live with the weight of remorse.

Then, on the other side of the coin, I often wonder how Vietnamese people living here now in America feel about us Vietnam Veterans. Are they grateful to us? Do they hate us? Do they understand why we did what we did? Can they ever forgive me? Can I ever forgive them? Can they sense my discomfort in being around them?

Until recently, I've never considered how my contributions to the war may have caused my former enemy's families to anguish over the loss of *their loved ones*, or struggled to provide care to a severely disabled relative from war wounds. Are Americans the *only ones* who struggle with PTSD? Did my actions cause them to also struggle with flashbacks and emotional numbness that caused them to also be emotionally absent fathers, husbands, or friends?

ARMY, BECAUSE NOBODY EVER PLAYED "NAVY" AS A KID

In 1965, my Brother was drafted into the Army and underwent training to become an infantry soldier. A few months later, he was home on leave prior to shipping out for his deployment to Vietnam. I listened with great interest and envy to his stories about his military training experiences and hilarious camaraderie antics. I loved hearing his stories about shouting cadence songs while marching and the thrill of getting to shoot rifles, pistols, and machine guns. I especially envied hearing about his heart-pounding experience of learning to throw live exploding hand grenades. I remember how cool I thought it was to try on his "REAL" Army uniform with all its shiny military pins, multi-colored patches, and ribbons. These were all the things we would mimic as kids when playing Army. The idea of getting to experience all that for real made me seriously consider joining the Army after graduating high school.

He would write home from Vietnam periodically but avoided sharing any details about the horrors of war that he was experiencing. I would later realize during my own deployment that his purpose was not to add more reasons for my parents to worry.

During my senior year of High School, I did only the bare minimum required to get my diploma. I was more interested in girls, singing in a rock band, and refurbishing my first car, a rusted 1956 Ford Sunliner convertible.

That August in 1966, I turned 18 years old. At that time, it was mandated by law that I register for the draft. Knowing that I probably wasn't going to take college academics seriously, I asked the people at the draft office when the next draft call was. They told me it would be the following month, so I said, "Put me on it."

About a week later, I received a notice in the mail ordering me to appear for induction into the Army at a processing center in downtown Oakland. I excitedly wrote my brother to tell him what I did. Instead of congratulating me, I received a scathing letter back from him, telling me what a foolish idiot I was. Since he was in the middle of the chaos of combat then, he tried to convince me that I had no clue about the horrific journey that lay ahead of me, and that he wished he could prevent me from experiencing it. The normal deployment during the Vietnam War was twelve months; he even volunteered to extend his tour of duty an additional six months in hopes that it would prevent me from having to go. He had heard there was a new law pending that prevented siblings from the same household from being sent to Nam within 12 months of each other. Unfortunately, that law passed after I had already been in Vietnam for about four months into my own deployment.

In September 1966, I reported to the Induction Center in Oakland as instructed, then boarded an airplane and flew to Fort Lewis, Washington, to begin my 10 weeks of basic training. My first night was spent cracking jokes with the rest of the new recruits until about 2 o'clock in the morning. Yes...4:30 A.M. came all too quickly when the lights came on, followed by our Drill Sergeant yelling profanities at us to wake up as garbage cans were being thrown down on the floor and kicked across the aisle between our bunks.

Basic Training was more than what my brother warned me about, and more than what the movie *The D.I.* starring Jack Webb in 1957 depicted. It was more getting yelled at, more push-ups, more marching, more getting yelled at, more getting rained on, more getting yelled at again. We had to wear our steel pots (helmet) everywhere, all the time, to strengthen our skinny teenage necks and get us used to having them on. This later proved to be a definite lifesaver for many of us in war.

⚜

Up to this point in my life, I had never even touched any kind of real gun. However, soon we were issued M-14 rifles. Before ever getting to shoot them, we were taught how to handle, drill with, dis-assemble, clean, then re-assemble them over and over until it became second nature to us. On one such occasion, after cleaning my rifle, I asked the Drill Sergeant for permission to return my "gun" to the "Gun Rack." He came right up to my face and hollered, "What the F*&@# did you call that?" I shivered back, "The gun rack Drill Sergeant." He leaned in right up to my face, and hollered back with spit spraying in my eyes, "That is not a gun, It's your rifle, your weapon, your piece." He then blurted out that old familiar military phrase, pointing to my M-14, "Repeat after me, THIS IS MY RIFLE," then pointing to my crotch, "THIS IS MY GUN," back at the rifle, "THIS IS FOR KILLING," then to my crotch again, "THIS IS FOR FUN." I had to repeat that drill 3 times and for punishment, every night I had to tuck my rifle into bed, kiss it goodnight, and sleep with it for the next 2 weeks.

There were other types of disciplinary forms of punishment besides the usual "push-up" or calisthenics. The worst and most brutal was called the Dying Cockroach. In full battle dress, you had to lie on your back (even in the pouring rain) with your legs and arms straight up in the air while holding your rifle, and your head off of the ground. You had to remain in this position until the Drill Sergeant was convinced that you suffered long enough in miserable pain and humiliation. It didn't take long for your legs to quiver and your stomach muscles to cramp from the weight of your combat boots. Next, your arms and shoulders would ache from holding up the 10-pound M-14 rifle, and your neck would burn from the strain of keeping your head off the ground while wearing your 3-4-pound steel helmet.

⚜

One time while standing in formation, someone from behind me threw a rock, hitting my helmet with a loud ping, so I spun around, ready to square off at the guy behind me. We both threw our helmets off and doubled up our fists, ready to mix it up. It was then that I recognized that he was Benji, my childhood friend whom I hadn't seen since we were 8 years old! Because our hair was now shaved short, we looked almost exactly like we did 10 years earlier. What a thrill it was to reconnect with him after all these years. We eventually both got reassigned to the same unit in Fort Hood, Texas, after graduating Basic. After several months of AIT there, we got deployed to Vietnam together again in the same unit. Much of our time together was spent talking about our home lives, including our cars and our girlfriends. We were always together, and soon we were referred to as "Nip and Flip" because Benji was Japanese and me being Filipino.

Devastatingly, Benji was killed in Vietnam. His loss, along with that of several others, was a huge factor in my hesitation or desire not to form any more close friendships during and after the war. It became a garden that took me several years to trust in and relearn how to cultivate.

GOING AWOL WAITING FOR MY BROTHER

After completing AIT at Fort Hood, prior to shipping out for Vietnam, we were all given two weeks' leave to spend with our loved ones. During my leave, I tried to spend as much time as possible with my High School Sweetheart, Jane, trying my best to memorize her face, her kisses, her voice, and her perfume. We made promises to write often and wait faithfully for my return home.

I also knew that my brother was due to return home any day from his tour in Vietnam. There was no way I was going to the Nam without seeing him, so I waited an *additional week past my leave time.* His phone call finally came to advise us that he was at the Oakland Army Base processing out of the Army. It was only about a half an hour's drive from home, so I jumped in my dad's car and drove to the O.A.B. to find him. Once found, I told him that we needed to go to the local Red Cross Office so that I could turn myself in for being a week AWOL! I told the person at the Red Cross office about my predicament and even showed him my brother and his Army exit papers. The Red Cross agent promptly phoned my Company Commander, Captain Brady, in Fort Hood, Texas, to confirm my situation, then handed me the phone so that I could speak to my Captain. To my relief and surprise, he understood and sympathized with my decision to refuse to go to war without first seeing my brother. He understood the high likelihood that a second child from the same household might not survive combat to return home. He told me he would excuse me from being AWOL and even gave me a couple more days' leave. However, with a firm warning, he *loudly added* that I'd better return for duty afterwards or face court-martial.

Since that day, I have had such high gratitude and respect for Captain Brady that I decided he was the kind of leader who was trustworthy enough that I would gladly follow him into battle and trust him with my life.

LEAVING FOR THE NAM

A week or two after reporting back to Fort Hood, after my leave and prior to being deployed to Vietnam, my whole division was flown to the Oakland Army Base, where we boarded an old WWII troop transport ship called the USNS Upshur. O.A.B. was so close to my home, but once on board, we weren't allowed to get off of the ship. It was so frustrating not to be able to visit my mother, who also ironically worked there.

It took several hours to load the tons of equipment and supplies and settle into our new surroundings. We were finally underway for South East Asia. It was such a mix of conflicting emotions to see the underside of the Golden

Gate Bridge as we sailed out of the San Francisco Bay beneath it, wondering if I would survive to return alive. As we headed into the open ocean, I gathered with several of my fellow soldiers on deck, looking over the rail of the ship to marvel at the waves crashing higher and higher on the depth markers that ran up the sides of the bow. The waves would splash higher and then lower, higher then lower, as the ocean swells became larger. Gradually, conversations quieted, and people started to disappear. Up and down, up and down, and I began to realize why. Yes, queasiness was setting in, and my efforts to swallow down my vomit became useless. I stayed seasick for two days straight, confirming that joining the Army instead of the Navy—my dad's suggestion—was the right choice.

Our quarters were down in the last few decks near the bottom of the ship. To make matters worse, both interior side walls converged in front of us, indicating that we were housed down at the bow of the ship. That's where the rocking motion of any ocean vessel is felt the most. On top of that, we found out we were in the middle of a storm.

It felt like being on an elevator as the bow rose up out of the water, then thundered as it came crashing back down into the angry ocean. Our bunks were made of canvas, tied by ropes around tubular metal frames, all stacked four high with only a foot or two between them. We had to lie flat to squeeze in and out of them. Needless to say, panic set in whenever the seasick person above you started to heave. The place began to *reek* of B.O., puke, and cigarette smoke.

Thankfully, the storm moved on a few days later, giving us the opportunity to go out on deck for some much-welcomed breaths of fresh air and sunshine. All we wanted to do was lie around and relax, but those in charge had other plans. Our days became filled with continuous rigorous sessions of P.T. (Physical Training, calisthenics), lifeboat drills, and repeatedly disassembling, cleaning, and then reassembling our rifles. It was the same numbing routine day after day, repeatedly, until 21 days later—land ho! Off in the distance, we saw the coastline of land—real land—rather than just endless ocean. Except for the droning hum of the ship's engine and the gentle lapping of the waves against the sides of our ship, a hush came over all of us as we realized that we were actually looking at the ominous land of Vietnam.

I remember the feeling of butterflies in my stomach and tightness in my throat, making me swallow hard to push down the fear that started to well up inside of me. For once, since being on this floating prison, I wished that I could just stay there on the ocean and not have to set foot on that ominous chunk of land that grew larger and more real with each passing minute. Then a voice blared over the intercom, informing us that we would soon arrive at the port of Da Nang, ordering us to go below, gather all of our gear, and prepare to disembark. Yikes! The dreaded "Vietnam" was frighteningly becoming more and more real. I looked around at the crowd of soldiers surrounding me and couldn't help but wonder which one of us would be returning home upright or in a flag-draped coffin. God, please don't let me be among the latter.

Once on dry land, the heat and humidity felt overwhelming. Sweat started to leak profusely from every pore, causing our fatigues to cling to our bodies as if we had just taken a hot shower in them. The air was hot and heavy, smelling like damp earth, wet vegetation, our sweat, and dead fish. Based on war movies that I watched growing up, I expected our landing to be like storming the beaches of Normandy with bullets and bombs blasting away. To my relief, the Port of Da Nang looked more like any other military harbor in America. No guns blazing, no bombs exploding, just unarmed soldiers busily operating cranes, forklifts, and various other military vehicles. We spent our first night in real barracks rather than sleeping on the ground or in tents as we had expected. We even ate dinner in a real mess hall with a choice of meat, fish, or chicken. There were even three flavors of ice cream for dessert. Nothing at all about this place felt like what I thought a war zone would be like. I thought to myself that being here might actually be a piece of cake. Soon enough, though, my assumption would prove false.

The next morning, we were herded onto LSTs (a large, heavy equipment Navy transport ship) and made our way down the coast to Chu Lai, which became our main base Headquarters. All of the sights and sounds there started to suggest that this was indeed more like what I thought a war-zone military base would look like. There were sandbag bunkers fronted by rows of barbed wire. Everyone carried weapons. All of the jeeps, trucks, helicopters, and tanks had machine guns mounted on them. Further out, artillery guns were frequently booming off fire missions, I suppose in support of troops outside the wire who were in contact and needed help. Not knowing that this was still a very secure base, I wondered why we still haven't been issued ammunition for these empty rifles we were carrying so that we could defend ourselves. It's been said that an empty rifle is nothing more than just a stick.

Soon we were crowded onto a convoy of duce and a half's (2 ½ ton military trucks) and driven down a dusty, bumpy, rust colored, clay dirt road to our soon-to-be Brigade Headquarters. It seemed as if anything that wasn't a green canvas tent or vegetation was that rust-colored clay dirt, the dust from which made all of the bunkers, tents, and vehicles look as if they were oxidizing. There, we were separated into our respective companies, then platoons, and assigned to large canvas tents to bunk down in.

IN COUNTRY

"FORT HOOD GI'S RIOT, REFUSING TO GO TO NAM"

I took my basic training in Fort Lewis, Washington. Then, in December 1966, I was reassigned to Fort Hood, Texas, for AIT (Advanced Individual Training) until being deployed to Vietnam the following September. After being in the Nam for a couple of months, a friend of mine, "back in the world" (home), sent me a copy of a popular underground anti-establishment newspaper at that time called *The Berkeley Barb*. On the front page in big bold letters, the headline read, "FORT HOOD G.I.s RIOT, REFUSING TO GO."

The truth, though, was that we weren't protesting having to go to Vietnam, we were just so sick and tired of being in that miserable, dusty, dry, rattlesnake-infested Fort Hood for over 9 months. The reality was that we were so over-joyed to finally be getting out of that Texas hellhole. We ended up partying so hard to the point of becoming extremely "drunk and disorderly."

The article grossly over exaggerated claims of us causing over $150,000 in property damage, panty raids on the WAC's barracks (there were no WAC's in Fort Hood at that time), even beating a Lieutenant to death, and more contributed to our "anti-war exuberance." It's funny how the media twisted it to say we were rioting about not wanting to go to Vietnam when, in truth, we were really just celebrating. I wish that I would have thought to keep that copy of the *Barb*. It would have made an interesting piece of memorabilia, but like several "souvenirs" that I discarded after getting home, they were only reminders of the year that I wanted desperately to forget.

I was, however, able to find a website that looks like basically the same over-exaggerated information from the original article. Evidentially, fake news existed even back then. I found it by

Googling: Library Reading Room, GI Riot Rocks Fort Hood. The Fort Hood Riots of October 3, 1967, by Pvt. "Scotty" Frame.

If you are curious, here is the URL for that article:
https://displacedfilms.com/sir-no-sir-archive/archives_and_resources/library/articles/bond_05.html

FIRST TO GET SHOT AT

We had been humping the bush in an area about 40 klicks West of Chu Lai all day, looking for any evidence of the enemy's presence. At this point, we were becoming hungry for our first taste of contact with the enemy. As the day wore on, we started our ascent of a hill to set up our night position. Upon reaching the hilltop, we got assigned defensive positions circling the hilltop with 3 men per position and started digging our foxholes. In spite of being exhausted from patrolling all day, then climbing uphill with 70 pounds of equipment on our backs, we still had the task of digging foxholes large and deep enough for three men to crouch down to sleep in and defend from. Not an easy task with rocky, hard dirt to dig in with small foldable Army-issued hand shovels.

Eventually, a supply helicopter arrived with cases of C-Rations, jerry cans of fresh drinking water, marmite cans of hot chow, and most importantly, mail from home. This being only our initial third or fourth week "in country," we were growing anxious to experience our first taste of a real firefight.

Johnson, Gary Amberson, and I shared a foxhole and took turns going to the center of our platoon's security perimeter, where our hot chow, water, mail, and extra ammo were being distributed. Amberson was the first to retrieve his goodies while Johnson and I stayed at our foxhole to keep an eye out for any enemy while completing the fortification of our position.

I felt the call of nature building up in my gut and told Johnson that I was going out a few yards out in front of our foxhole to "do my business." I reminded him to be sure and let Amberson know that I was out there in front before he left to get his food and mail. As I finished pulling up my pants and reached for my rifle, I hear Gary frantically start yelling, "VC, I got one, VC, VC !!!!" followed by the "kack-kack-kack-kack-kack" barking of his M-60 machine gun. Dirt was kicking up all around me, and shredded bits of vegetation rained down on me like confetti.

It became horribly obvious that I was the one Gary was shooting at.

Evidently, in his anxiousness to get his food and mail, Johnson forgot to tell Amberson where I was. I lay as flat on my back as I could, but the 60 wouldn't let up. I kept yelling, "Cease fire, fire cease, it's me you idiot" over and over but the barking of the 60 and him yelling, "I got one, I got one" drowned out my desperate pleas for recognition.

I can still clearly remember feeling the heat of the tracer bullets and the smell of spent gun powder cracking just above my nose. Dirt and broken pieces of vegetation rained down all over me and stuck to my sweaty face and arms. During machine gun training, we were instructed to fire no more than six rounds at a time to avoid overheating the weapon, which would cause it to malfunction. A full can of M-60 ammo holds about 250 rounds of 7.62mm rounds belted together.

Obviously, Gary's training must have gotten lost in his excitement to finally get to shoot at a live target. Rather than burst of six rounds at a time, he just hung on to the trigger, discharging one long continuous eruption of bullets. The only part of his training he did exceptionally well was to quickly reload another belt of ammo into the 60 without skipping a beat. By this time, the rest of our perimeter started shooting blindly into the trees and bushes in front of them.

After firing several hundred rounds at my position, Gary's machine gun finally went silent. I seized this opportunity to start yelling to him again. Finally, he yelled back, "Tony, is that you?" He started laughing hysterically from the horror of realizing the tragedy that had come so close to happening.

I screamed back, "You could have killed me, you crazy #$%^^$#@!" All throughout our perimeter, men were hollering, "Cease fire, cease fire! What the hell is everyone shooting at?" Final assessment proved that it was just a case of "itchy trigger fingers" launched by Amberson's hunger to be the first to get a "Dink."

It turns out that the only reason Gary stopped shooting was because the barrel of his machine gun got so hot that the glowing red barrel warped so badly that it ceased to function! Since I was the first man in our platoon to get shot at, most everyone would excitedly ask me what it's like to get shot at. My only response was, "Trust me, JUST DON'T GET SHOT AT." Thankfully, during the shooting, there was just enough of a dirt mound for me to lay flat on my back behind. I am convinced that the fact that I was a little skinny, 128 lb. guy helped to make me a small, harder-to-hit target. By the grace of God, had Gary been able to continue shooting, that little dirt mound would eventually have been whittled down to my grave.

Little did I realize that this was just the first of many times that I would experience being shot at.

⚜

It didn't take very long to become familiar with the sound of bullets flying past me. When bullets streak past you, they make a distinct "snap" or "crack" sound similar to the sonic boom from a jet passing overhead at supersonic speed. Since a bullet is much smaller, its "sonic boom" is just a "crack" or "snap" sound, followed by a faint "pop." The pop comes from the gun that fired the shot. This helps determine which way the shot came from. The longer the gap between the "snap" and the "pop," the farther away the shooter is. The more immediate the "pop" sound happens after the "snap," the closer the shooter is, so you had better be ready to engage your adversary. Hollywood seems to always portray bullet sounds as a zing or whirling sound, not true! That sound comes only from a ricochet that causes a bullet to tumble. The bullet has either glanced off a rock, a tree, or a human body. However, a direct hit on a body sounds more like a handful of raw ground beef smacking up against the wall, followed by a grunt, scream, or a cry of profanity.

To this day, Amberson and I stay in frequent touch with each other. When we talk, we always joke about that incident, and now the amount of rounds shot at me is up to an exaggerated 600 plus. A few years ago, Gary had a T-shirt made for me with my Army picture on it and the words, "First man I ever shot at, last man I ever missed." No truer words could be said because Gary became an exceptionally skilled gunner, valiantly saving many of our butts during desperate situations, mine included several times!!!

Then there is "The Bean." We dubbed him the name "Bean" because of his last name, Stringham. We couldn't call him "StringBEAN" because he wasn't skinny and appeared to be well-fed. So, just "Bean" seemed the most appropriate. He eventually earned his way up to becoming our Platoon Sergeant. To this day, I jokingly talk smack to him for frequently choosing me to walk point, or crawl into tunnels, or going off by myself to be a security night listening observer. The truth is that he had keen instincts for sensing when and how to use the right man for the proper situations and when it was or wasn't safe to do so. For his excellent care for his men and gallant actions under fire, Bean was awarded one Silver Star, four

Bronze Stars, and three Purple Hearts. I am so thankful to God that all three of us have been able to remain extremely close friends and in frequent contact with each other after all these years. I will forever cherish these two men with the highest degree of respect, admiration, and love. I'm alive and here to share my story thanks to both of these gallant men.

VIET CONG TACTICS

In World Wars I and II, the progress of victory was measured by territory taken or won back from our enemies. Battle lines were drawn, and all territory behind was safely controlled by allied forces. All of the territory in front of the battle line was occupied and controlled by the opposing enemy forces. Both friendly and opposing soldiers were easily identified by distinctive uniforms worn by each fighting force.

The Vietnam War was much different in that there were *no distinctive* battle lines. The Viet Cong were everywhere and wore *no identifiable* uniform. It was easy for them to blend in with all of the other population as just normal farmers, merchants, or other members of civilian men, women, and children. The customary attire of most of the indigenous population was black pajama-like clothing, bare feet or sandals, and a broad cone-shaped straw hat. The only way to identify them as the "enemy" was when they shot at us or tried to blow us up. The Viet Cong usually fought with small, swift "hit and disappear" guerrilla-type tactics. The only uniformed enemy we encountered was the NVA (North Vietnam Army) who infiltrated into South Vietnam. The NVA were better armed and trained soldiers from Communist North Vietnam. They wore khaki colored uniforms with pith helmets and fought against us in larger, organized numbers. They often engaged us in more ferocious and prolonged battles. However, like the Viet Cong, they also would break off contact after inflicting casualties on us and disappear deep into the jungle. Because there were no clear battle lines in Vietnam, the only way to determine any measurable progress in our efforts was by "body count." In other words, the more we killed, the more victorious we became. Soon enough, the honeymoon would be over, and our first taste of an actual firefight would become an unpleasant aftertaste. More often than not, one or two Viet Cong would snipe at us, then disappear into the dense vegetation, baiting us to launch an aggressive chase after them. Sometimes we lost track of them, other times we only found bloody trails that led off into the jungle. Once in a great while, though, we got lucky and found bodies. Through decades of fighting, Charlie (Viet Cong, VC, Victor Charles) had become superior at jungle and guerrilla warfare. His hit-and-run tactic gave him the opportunity to study our habits and design his strategies against us. He observed how we would all go chase after one or two snipers, then lay our weapons down to relax, joke, smoke, or eat once we mistakenly felt that the threat was averted. Armed with this knowledge, Charlie would then launch a larger manned attack, catching us totally unprepared to rapidly defend ourselves.

Combat lesson #1: always, always, always stay vigilant and never, never, never completely relax.

Combat lesson #2: keep plenty of ammo on

you and your weapon, no more than half an arm's length away. If not, people die!

I learned Lesson #1 so well by practicing it 24/7 for 365 days without ceasing that I have not been able to completely unlearn, and I remain ultra-vigilant, even now. Still, even to this day, while driving through the countryside, I catch myself watching for possible places that look like potential ambush sites.

Sometimes, our own mind became the enemy, especially at night while trying to stay awake during security watch. Fear, fatigue, and lack of adequate sleep became a perfect storm for mind tricks. Sounds, smells, and shadows all become suspicious, so you stare in a feeble attempt to confirm whether it's just your imagination or if that bush is really moving towards you. All the while, your eyes are begging for just a few seconds to shut and rest. Charlie knew how to hunt us and studied our habits to identify our weaknesses. He's had decades of wars to perfect his tactics and dig complex tunnel systems in which to make himself invisibly immune to our bombs and bullets. He has learned how to be sneaky, fight dirty, with no such thing as fighting fair.

We quickly realized that the only way to defeat and demoralize this type of enemy is through continuous, overwhelming, violent aggression. Sadly, our political leaders would restrict our capabilities to do so with "Rules of Engagement," "No Fire Zones," "Border Crossing Restrictions," and various other so-called restrictions on "inhumane" or "politically incorrect" tactics.

It is also my personal experience that war protestors are responsible for many of the names on the Vietnam Memorial Wall. Their protests and riots only served to compel the politicians to impose ridiculous "Rules of Engagement" on us warriors in order to placate the protestors. Small stealth units of us were sometimes sent on covert missions to sneak into Laos to only confirm suspected supply routes used by the North Vietnamese insurgents, so that B-52 Bombers could be called in to destroy those supply routes and it's users. Sometimes our presence would be discovered and overwhelmed by their superior numbers. Those situations left us unable to get any of our air or artillery support until we could hastily make our way back across the border. We often had no choice but to leave our dead and severely wounded behind.

We haven't been allowed to win a war since World War II. Yet they continue to send us off to fight, bleed, and die without full unrestricted support, only to withdraw and go home with no real victory or sense of accomplishment. It's as if they confuse war with practicing "pull-out" birth control.

BETTER HIM THAN ME

One question that combat veterans detest hearing is, "What is it like to shoot someone?" or "How many did you kill?" It's extremely difficult to answer honestly because, to do so, one must relive the reality of actually having done it, sometimes unintentionally, not just once but multiple times, without remorse or regret. I truly would prefer not to address these questions, but my reason for writing this book makes it a relevant necessity.

All combat veterans deal with memories of taking lives differently. Some can talk it out; others completely refuse to acknowledge it. For me, I'm still not proud of having done it; I'm just thankful for surviving it and that it no longer *tries* to define me. I do have deep remorse for having done it as a result of "friendly fire" accidents or "collateral damage" incidents. Instead of acknowledging how many lives I have taken, I prefer to focus on how many *more lives I've saved*. I credit my ability to speak about this publicly now, thanks to the circle of support I've been blessed with—Veteran support groups, my spiritual brothers from church, and especially my wife, who can recognize "the look" and knows exactly how to pray and talk me back out from the jungle. Also, largely, thanks to several truth-filled bible verses like:

John 8:31-32

"If you abide in My word, you are truly My disciples, then you will know the truth,
and the truth will set you free."

So here goes. Most exchanges during a firefight with the enemy involved all of us grunts firing towards the general direction of a threat while frantically ducking for cover, dodging or diving to alternating shooting positions, or calling for artillery or air support. Those situations often produced body counts, but couldn't confirm who or what should actually be credited with ending the lives of the threat's instigators.

The first time I actually saw someone I had dropped, was on February 8, 1968, in the Battle of Lo Giang during the Tet Offensive. This was our first contact with North Vietnam Regular Army soldiers. Unlike skirmishes with small groups of "hit and run" Viet Cong, the NVA fought aggressively with larger, organized units. They were highly experienced, very tenacious, and well-equipped soldiers from North Vietnam. My squad was the lead element of our platoon that day.

We were crossing an open rice paddy nearing the tree line on the opposite end when the whole tree line opened up on us like a fire-breathing dragon. My point-man, Tankersley, "Tank," was immediately hit and dropped down into the cover of the knee-high rice reeds. He kept screaming my name and frantically yelling, "I'm hit, I'm hit, oh God...Tony, I'm hit," over and over.

I peeked up from my place of cover and saw his hand waving above the tops of the reeds, crimson red with his own blood. Somehow, through the blizzard of bullets, I was able to sprint, duck, shoot, and dive my way over to his writhing, bloody body. Every time I attempted to lift my head up to assess our surroundings, bullets from the tree line would crack past my ears.

Another guy from my squad, "Jimmy," amazingly, without getting hit, made his way to us through the hurricane of full-metal-jacketed, demon-like bees. He peeked up over the rice paddy dike in an attempt to target someone to shoot at.

Just as I yelled at him to keep his head down, I heard what sounded like a handful of raw hamburger meat smacking up against a wall. His head jerked backwards as a pinkish mist billowed out from the back of his neck. He got shot through his open mouth. He slowly turned his head and looked straight into my eyes and weakly gurgled, "My mmouthhhhhh," lowered his head onto my right elbow as blood spilled from his mouth and his last breath hissed out from his lungs.

That was the first of many times to come that someone died in my arms. It was also the first time I had to close a dead man's lifeless eyes. Not because it is the customary thing to do, but because I couldn't stand having his hauntingly motionless blue eyes staring at me.

The exact details of when or how our medic got over to us are blurry. I just recall that it took two or three doses of morphine to get Tank to stop screaming. All the while, bullets kept snapping and zinging over our heads from the tree line in front of us and from my fellow soldiers behind us, who didn't realize we were in front of them. This made it impossible to move out of our position to seek safety and get Tank and Jimmy onto a Medivac chopper with the rest of the increasing number of dead and wounded.

All we could do was lie as flat as possible under the nose-high ceiling of bullets ripping through the air over us from both directions. There was no way I could even participate in the fight, just lying there trying to be as small as possible, wondering if this was the day I die. We couldn't even raise our hands up high enough to wave off our guys from shooting over us. This was bad, really, *REALLY BAD!* There's no way it could get worse....WRONG !!!

Hunkered down on our backs, the only clear vision we had was of the sky. In utter horror, we saw one of our Cobra gunship helicopters diving un-mistakenly straight towards our open position in the rice paddy, with machine guns and rockets blasting away. "My God, he's shooting at us!" Doc and I screamed. We shouted at the top of our lungs to "Stand down, cease fire, hey, we're Americans, you idiot!" Our pleas for help were uselessly drowned out by all of the gunfire and explosions going on all around us in every conceivable direction.

As misfortune would have it, our incompetent Platoon Lieutenant was not able to inform the gunship of our location because he was hiding behind cover, calling for air strikes, but not able to watch where it was hitting. Deafening explosions and machine gun rounds from the Cobra's assault on us were going off all around us, causing rice paddy water and huge football-sized clumps of mud to rain down on us. We did our best to use Jimmy's body as a shield. Miraculously, somehow the three of us survived that initial strafing but noticed the gunship turning to make another run at our position.

In a panic, the only thing we could think to do was to open a large field bandage and use Tank's blood to smear a big red cross on it. Lying on our backs as flat as possible, we held the opened bandage over our chests. As the gunship turned on final approach at us, he must have finally noticed our signal because the chopper jerked into a hard right climb and disappeared into the smoke-filled sky. I don't know how long I had been holding my breath, but I quickly sucked in a huge gulp of air and then gradually exhaled as my rigid body relaxed and deflated back into the mud.

Much of what followed was just a blur caused by the flood of adrenaline in me. All I recall is that we fought our way back to where a medivac helicopter was picking up our dead and wounded. We loaded Tank's blood-soaked body and Jimmy's lifeless, dead weight onto the floor of the chopper. I wanted to run and hide somewhere to cry and vomit, but was also so full of anger, horror, and rage that instead, I turned around and ran to rejoin the fight and get some payback.

Back in the rice paddy, I lifted my head up over a rice paddy dike that concealed my position and saw an NVA soldier crouching and scooting from the cover of one tree to another while relentlessly shooting to kill me. I lifted the stock of my rifle up to my cheek, peeked through the rear sight of my M16, aligned it with the front sight, focused in on his exposed silhouette, and emptied a full magazine into him on full auto. I'll forever remember how he twitched and flailed like a marionette puppet whose strings were getting cut one by one as my bullets ripped into his body, shattering his limbs and torso just prior to collapsing into a torn-up, twisted, bloody heap on the ground.

So, "How did it feel?" In all honesty, it was such an exhilarating high. I felt so victorious, so justified. Please try to understand that in the heat of battle, kill or be killed is the purest form of truth. Adrenaline floods your nervous system, fueling a desperate drive to survive. Added to it, the hurt, anger, and hunger for revenge from having just witnessed the death and mutilation of my two close friends, further infected any humane emotions I may have had with rabies-like rage.

Pass judgment on me if you want, but we had a saying in Nam:

"For those of us who have fought for it, life and death have a meaning the protected will never know."

I was _NOT_ celebrating the taking of a life. I was merely ecstatic at not losing mine. Better him than me! Then I said to myself, "That was for what you did to Jimmy and Tank, you S.O.B. I felt bad about killing him for about 10 seconds. That's about how long it took before more bullets started cracking and zinging all around me from someone else trying to kill me. "Sh—t!!!, no time to dwell on what just happened to Jimmy and Tank, better reload quick and get back into the fight or lay here and die!!!"

That was the day that I started to discard having a conscience.

We had sayings that we would repeat over and over to choke down any sickening, savage emotions. We would often refer to unpleasant experiences as "What a bring-down," followed by either saying "F— it, no sweat" or simply, "It don't mean nuthin." The sooner you can numb up, the sooner you can function as a combat soldier, without mercy, compassion, or remorse. Numbing up is essential to being able to do whatever it takes to move on, lead, fight, and survive without hesitation. In hindsight, those kinds of numbing expressions only served to protect our hearts behind an ever-thickening barricade fortified with mental sandbags.

Losing friends repeatedly during my tour of duty became far too painful. I reached a point where I no longer cared about making new friends or knowing any personal details about the new replacements. I only needed to know whether I could depend on them to function under fire or to stay awake during their turn for night watch. I only needed to know their names to give orders or if I had to identify their bodies and gather their few personal belongings to be sent home to their loved ones. The mantra "It don't mean nuthin" is the most tragic "double negative" in combat. It always ends up meaning everything that suffocates your emotional civility.

WHISKEY TANGO FOXTROT

In the military, when communicating on the radio, you would have to use the military phonetic alphabet to communicate with the receiving party. This helped to avoid misunderstanding important information. In other words, A was Alpha, B was Bravo, and C was Charlie. If a location was North East, you would say November-Echo; South West was Sierra Whisky, and so on. Saying profanity over the air was not allowed. However, grunts would always find ways to usurp protocol, especially when more dramatic emphasis was desired. Thus, when an undesirable order was given or a really bad decision was made, we said, "Whiskey Tango Foxtrot," which simply meant "What the (F-bomb)!!!"

As my tour progressed in Vietnam, I found myself being temporarily on loan to other platoons in our Company due to attrition to their leadership ranks from battle casualties. I took over leading squads in the 1st, 2nd, and 4th Platoons from time to time to help cover gaps in their Squad Leader positions while helping to train new replacements. One night, when I was finally back with my 3rd Platoon, we were struggling to move quietly through waist-high brush. The evening sky was overcast, making it extremely dark and hard to navigate our direction of travel while attempting to minimize all of the crackling noises we were making stepping through the tangling maze. However, I recognized the terrain since I had been through there previously while on loan to the 1st Platoon. I decided to make my way up to Captain Brady so that I could inform him that I knew of a trail about fifty yards off to our left that we could use to get out of the noisy brush that we were in. He appreciated my advice and told me to lead the way. I took point, and the rest of the company followed. We carefully made our way to the trail.

Once on the trail, the going became much easier, and thankfully, the cloudy night sky began to break up slightly, giving us tiny bits of moonlight to help me see ahead. The brush that lined the sides of the trail started to become taller and taller until it was about head high. The thought occurred to me that this was becoming too ideal a place for us to walk into an ambush, so I silently raised my closed fist to signal for the column of men behind me to halt.

Instinctively, they got low with their weapons, alternately pointing left and right. Just then, I heard a rustling in the bushes ahead on my right, so I knelt down on one knee, clicked the safety on my rifle off, and raised it to my shoulder. I could barely make out the silhouette of a rifle poking out from the bush, followed by an arm, and then a body that completely emerged into the open. With my heart pounding rapidly in my throat, I swallowed hard, took a deep breath, and quickly rattled off three rounds center mass and then lay down flat in case there was return fire. The body grunted and moaned as it collapsed to the ground, and I waited for what seemed like an eternity until

I felt it seemed safe to move forward to assess the situation.

Slowly and quietly, I stepped forward in a crouch until I reached the body. In the dim shadows, I was horrified to discover it was *Captain Brady!* I signaled for the guys behind me to move up to my position. When they joined me, in agony, I managed to choke out the words, "My God, it's Brady. I didn't know it was the Captain! Is he dead?!!!" Suddenly, a voice frantically cried out from inside the bushes, "Don't shoot, don't shoot!!" I spun around and pointed my weapon toward the sound of that voice and demanded that he come out and identify himself. It was "Screech," the Captain's radioman, who had been pointing his rifle at my head, ready to fire until he recognized my voice and came out of the bushes.

Our medic started administering aid to the Captain and advised Screech to quickly call for a medivac. Miraculously, my shots were slightly low and missed hitting any vital organs. I later found out that two rounds hit him in his abdomen, and the third hit him in the groin..

Because it was a friendly fire incident, I was ordered to board the medivac chopper with the Captain so that the circumstances of the shooting could be investigated back at base camp headquarters. Prior to being shipped to the hospital at Chu Lai, I was granted permission to visit Captain Brady in the surgery unit. In his groggy, half-conscious state, he was able to admit that it was his bad decision for him and his radioman to continue pushing straight forward through the brush so that they could rendezvous with the rest of us on the trail. For some dumb reason, though, he failed to let the rest of us know. "WHAT THE **W**HISKEY **T**ANGO **F**OXTROT, **were you thinking, Sir!!!**"

Even in his foggy condition, he remained true to his compassionate leadership style by trying to console my remorseful apologies by repeating over and over that it was *his fault,* and not mine. The investigation determined that the shooting did not happen because of any negligence on my part. Nevertheless, I realized I was the one responsible for shooting off his ability to father any children, and I paralyzed him from the waist down for the *rest of his life*. For the time being, it made me never want to shoot or even touch a gun ever again. Regardless, after reviewing the details of the shooting and undergoing a psychiatric evaluation, I was deemed fit to return for duty and ordered to rejoin my unit back out in the field. Tragically, about a decade later, I heard rumors that he had committed suicide because he refused to live without the use of his legs or give his wife any children as a result of his own "bad" decision.

Several more sandbags packed onto my aching heart's emotional bunker.

This incident was just another one of my many extremely unpleasant experiences from the war that I will be sharing with you in the coming chapters. Looking back, I have to credit my loving God for covering me with the strength, grace, and mercy to live with the heavy burden of being the one who pulled the trigger that horrible night.

HIT FROM BEHIND

There was another time when we entered a small clearing with a few bamboo huts after traversing dense vegetation. Our new Company Commander, Captain Hernandez, who replaced Captain Brady, told me to pass the word to set up a security perimeter around the edges of the area and pick a spot in the center for his C.P. (Command Post or position) while he investigated what appeared to be a trip wire for a possible booby trap. I walked off and dropped my ruck sack (large nylon backpack supported by an aluminum frame) next to some trees for his CP a few yards away, then turned to relay his instructions to the rest of the troops. All of a sudden, there was a huge explosion, and I felt a heavy thump slam into my back, throwing me forward and onto the ground. The Captain had accidentally set off the booby-trapped unexploded artillery round. The impact knocked the wind out of me, and I was temporarily disoriented from the shock wave, unable to hear or see through the thick cloud of dirt, dust, and smoke. I couldn't feel if had been wounded or possibly dying, just numb and stunned. I remember how panic started to set in at the thought that maybe today was going to be **the day** that I die, and angry at the thought that the VC finally got me.

Eventually, the dust started to dissipate, and faint sounds of yelling and screaming started to get louder and louder. As I coughed the smoky dust from my lungs, I realized that our Medic was frantically trying to rouse me to assess my condition because my back was soaked with blood and chunks of flesh. Thankfully, he was able to determine that I wasn't injured, but that the mess on my back was from getting hit from behind by a large part of the Captain's torso, caused by the explosion. That is what slammed into me as I was walking away.

Once I was able to gather my wits, we had to begin the gruesome task of gathering up what body parts and gear we could find and place them in a rain poncho for extraction with the other KIA and WIA men. I found a bloody boot still containing a foot with its splintered tibia sticking out of it. Several feet further on, I picked up a helmet by its strap as a steaming pinkish-grey goo that smelled like burnt hair spilled out onto the toe of my boot.

Once again, numbing up was my go-to emotional pain killer, my only normal. "IT DON'T MEAN NUTHIN!!"..... more sandbags added to my anguishing heart's fortress.

TOO NUMB, TOO HUNGRY

On another occasion, we had been on patrol all day since early morning and came under fire as we neared a small rickety bamboo compound. We started catching heavy fire from every hut, so we withdrew to some cover while returning fire and simply called in for artillery support. As usual, "Arty" was right on target. The gunfire from the now destroyed and smoldering huts fell silent. So we moved back in to assess the damage. We found a few bodies, various weapons, and several blood trails leading away and off into the surrounding vegetation.

It was already about 1530 hours, and we hadn't had a chance to eat all day. Gary Amberson (the same guy who shot at me previously with his M60 machine gun) and I knew that we would soon be heading out to set up somewhere else for the night, so we had better steal this opportunity to open a couple of C-Rations cans and eat while we had the brief window to replenish our strength. As we sat on a log eating, we noticed that there was a dead VC woman's body off to our right, her black PJs still smoldering from being on fire. We just looked at each other, grunted, shrugged our shoulders, said to each other, "Bummer," then kept on eating while we still had the slim opportunity before moving on.

Normally, who in their right, civilized mind could even consider eating near a smoldering, dead body? The mantra of "It don't mean nothin," had already embedded itself into our young minds. We simply congratulated each other for helping to end that particular gene pool and for having the wisdom to eat upwind from her body…. more sandbags to fortify the ever-growing barricade around my heart.

The reality of war, with its unending daily doses of death, pain, fear, anger, sorrow, and extreme fatigue, became the centerpiece of my existence. It surrounded me no matter which direction I tried to look away, and shattered my illusion of "Life is precious." Today's youth are so disillusioned with video games and the ability to hit a reset button to start all over again. It has to have a numbing effect on their ability to fully comprehend the finality of death or dismemberment. Unlike the movies where people are neatly shot, leaving just a couple of small bullet holes and a few blood stains on their clothing, the reality is all sorts of gory, bloody body parts, shattered bones, steaming intestines, pools of slippery blood, and grotesquely disfigured faces. Most small arm wounds were from head shots because your face is usually the only exposed body part when you're looking for what to shoot at. Explosions from mortars, bombs, or artillery rounds are the most brutal because they produce indiscriminate chunks of hot, jagged, sharp pieces of metal flying in all directions. Shrapnel from these exploding demons are like hundreds of various-sized, white hot buzz saw blades that amputate limbs and rip open gaping holes in a human body, exposing mutilated bones, muscles, vessels, and organs. It's like being tossed into a blender that gets turned on, then off quickly. Some of us will get chopped up while others don't. There's no way to determine who will and who won't, nor how to prevent it. I decided that if it's my time to get "it," I'm going to get it. It won't even matter if I've taken cover behind a large boulder-when your time is up, it's up. I made up my mind that if that was the case, Charlie is going to have to earn my demise, but in the meantime, I'll take as many down with me as I can. I resolved to just be as fierce as I can for as long as I was able.

I am often asked which war movie most resembles real combat. Honestly though, nothing can really capture it all, but I'd say that *Platoon* gets close to the heart pounding spookiness of the night, the opening beach scene of *Saving Private Ryan* illustrates the desperation and chaos when there is a lack of adequate places to find cover from explosions and a hail of bullets, and *Hacksaw Ridge* comes a little closer for the carnage. However, none can truly capture the deafening explosions, agonizing screams, the crack or zing of bullets, or the smell of dirt, explosives, and blood.

At this point, I have chosen to forgo describing more examples of gore from my personal combat experiences in the hope that I've made my point and possibly painted you a more vivid image of what war is really like. Perhaps this has given you more insight into the reasons why we often choose not to talk about "the war."

These are just a few examples of the daily, weekly, and monthly savagery of war. I apologize for being so descriptive, but I think it is important that you understand the weightiness of the price we endured for the safety and freedoms of our loved ones back home. More importantly, why many of us have had such difficulties readjusting to civilized ways of living, loving, and maintaining meaningful relationships. We've seen, done, and endured the worst of human behavior.

On top of all that, life in the bush is also filled with many non-insurgent hazards and inconveniences. It's not enough to be fighting an enemy who is trying to kill you. There is also the never-ending battle against mosquitoes, leeches, spiders, snakes, even tigers and angry water buffalo. It seems like every living creature in this hellish place is just waiting for a chance to take you out of the fight.

And then there is hygiene, or rather, the lack of it. Keeping my rifle clean with the help of my toothbrush seemed a more practical trade-off. My life depended more on my weapon than my teeth, unless I might have to bite my foe if I ever had the misfortune of being engaged in hand-to-hand combat. Luckily, I always carried an ample supply of ammunition. My rationale was that shooting someone was far more effective than trying to stab, punch, or bite the enemy to death. Besides, a finger and a little bit of spit seemed adequate to rub away most of the grit off my teeth.

And of course, then there's "when nature calls." Obviously, there are no toilets or urinals when you're out in the bush. Keep in mind that back then, the infantry was not co-ed, so modesty was never a consideration when it came to relieving oneself. The bush always provided plenty of places to go #1. We all carried a foldable portable shovel-useful for digging foxholes, filling sandbags, sometimes as a weapon, but also for digging a small six-inch-deep hole for going #2. Back inside the wire, in a secure base camp, LZ compound, or outpost, we had the luxury of wooden structures affectionately called latrines. They were enclosed outhouses with screened windows for much-needed ventilation and usually had openings to comfortably seat 3 to 6 users at a time. Beneath each "seat," 55-gallon cans previously used to store Agent Orange were cut in half and placed strategically under every hole to catch each person's personal "donation." Eventually, those capture cans would quickly fill. The extremely unpleasant task of disposing of the waste was usually "volunTOLD" to the lowest ranking soldier or anyone who needed punitive discipline. It was referred to as "Sh— burning detail," which involved pulling each can out by hand from under the latrine, pouring gasoline into it, then lighting the contents on fire. The problem is that the fuel usually just floated on top of the waste, so the unlucky Sh—burning Technician had to continuously stir the contents with a long wooden pole to ensure that the gasoline mixed with the waste and toilet paper to burn it all up thoroughly. Of course, additional amounts of gasoline were periodically needed to keep the cremation of the "BBQ" going. Just like a campfire, no matter where you stood while stirring, the smoke and smell was inescapable! In most cases, this was a day-long process, after which no one wanted to come near you to avoid the stench. Early on in my tour, I had the misfortune of having to do the burn a couple of times. Fortunately, I quickly moved up in rank and got to nominate some other poor grunt to "do the burn."

In more recent times, my daughters have wondered why I've refused to change my grandchildren's dirty diapers. I guess I should have explained to them that the last time I burned poop, I vowed that I would never ever look at or smell someone else's poo ever again. However, payback time came years later when I had to take care of my brother, who had several health issues caused by Agent Orange exposure and became unable to care for himself. Agent Orange is no joke, and it took his life decades later after his service in the Vietnam War. I, too, have health issues from frequent exposure to Agent Orange.

◆

One mission required our unit to search a densely vegetated area along the Laotian border, suspected of hidden trails used by the North Vietnam insurgents to sneak supplies and equipment into South Vietnam. The dense vegetation made it impossible to perform reconnaissance by our aircraft. We radioed in the coordinates of the trails we discovered and waited for airplanes to spray the area with Agent Orange to kill the vegetation that concealed the trail's location. As the tankers approached, we were advised to lay face down, hold our breaths and cover our exposed necks with our hands to avoid any possible over-spray. Once the aircraft completed its pass over us, I remember getting up and having to wipe off the oily film covering my forearms. Of course, there were also those times back in base camps using the latrines while sitting above those recycled Agent Orange containers. Thank God, my side effects from those carcinogenic exposures, so far, are not as severe as my brother's. Nonetheless, my health issues today require me to take a handful of prescription medications twice per day in order to stay asymptomatic.

-♦-

As I recall, the longest we ever went without a real soap and water shower was 42 days. During this particular time, we were constantly patrolling and fighting so often that being back at any basecamp was only a distant dream. Whenever we came across a little bit of water, whether it was a flooded, dirty rice paddy or murky creek, it was an opportunity to quickly scoop up a handful of that nasty liquid and splash it onto our faces and necks. No time to stop, but just keep moving on. Eventually, the pores on my back would become so clogged with gunk that it felt like dozens of needles pricking me as my skin tried to push out the much-needed perspiration. The only positive was that at least the mosquitoes probably didn't like the way I tasted anymore.

-♦-

In the jungle, your eyes, ears, and nose were the three most valuable senses you possessed to alert you to any impending dangers. However, the monsoon season rendered them nearly useless with the never-ending roar of the downpours crashing onto the vegetation that always seemed to engulf us. Being continuously soaked was miserable, especially wet feet. In the bush, your feet are your sole mode of transportation, so keeping them in functioning condition was paramount. Whenever you had an opportunity to pause long enough to change socks, you'd take them off, ring them out, and powder your feet. Then you would put them over your shoulders under your shirt so that your body heat would partially dry and warm them. Then place the other semi-dry pair that you previously had under your shirt on your cold, wrinkled feet.

In November, there was a brief break in the rain just long enough to get a supply chopper out to us on a hilltop in the bush. Headquarters even made an attempt to bring us out some hot chow to remind us that it was Thanksgiving Day. We had no idea because in the bush, every day is just like any other. "It don't mean nothing." It seemed like a nice gesture, but the meal consisted of a piece of rain-soaked bread with a slice of cold turkey topped with a scoop of runny mashed potatoes, served on a soggy copy of the Stars and Stripes newspaper. I'll just say that it was, and probably still is, my most memorable Thanksgiving meal, even to this day.

.♦.

Our Platoon's call sign should have been "Charlie 3 Bait" because we were often "Volun-TOLD" to go on missions to investigate suspected enemy presence in certain areas. What this really meant was: go there to investigate if intelligence reports were correct, and if we got shot at, the intel was correct. We called it "Recon by fire." It's like putting your hand on a stove to see if it is hot; if you burn your hand, yep, it's hot.

Not all scars are from physical wounds. Sometimes they are from what's called "Survivor's guilt." My first was on 16 March 1968. That was the day that my childhood friend, Benji, was killed and my cherished friend, Gary Amberson, was severely wounded by a booby trap explosion. I was on a 3-day in-country R&R leave from combat, relaxing, decompressing, and having a little overdue fun. It wasn't until I returned to my unit feeling refreshed and re-energized that I was told what had happened to Benji and Gary.

A crushing feeling of loss and guilt flooded my emotions with the realization that I was off having a good time out of harm's way, while tragedy took out the two people who had saved my life on several occasions and meant the world to me. Perhaps if I had been there with them, I might have been able to somehow help prevent them from missing the tripwire before they walked through and triggered it..... More sandbags added to the ever-thickening protective fortification around my scarred heart.

Gary's wounds were very severe, and I didn't know if he was able to survive them, and to find out that he didn't would have been far too painful to know. I simply avoided inquiring about his status, and to spare myself from devastating sorrow, I chose to completely put the question out of my mind. Surprisingly, in the fall of 2000, Bean located him and gave him my phone number. I was so shocked but elated to find out that Gary was still alive and reunited with him in 2001. The three of us have since gotten together annually for a reunion.

It wasn't until our third or fourth reunion that Gary finally felt able to share the details of March 16, 1968, with Bean and me. He said that he landed about 10 feet away from Benji from the explosion. He was able to see that Benji's wounds weren't going to be survivable, but worse yet, a tear gas grenade that he always carried was ignited by the explosion, and now, sitting on Benji's chest, suffocating him and denying his attempts to inhale his last few breaths and voice his desperate need for help. Gary's stomach was ripped open from the shrapnel and unable to move. He wanted desperately to knock the grenade off of Benji so that he could breathe, but all he could do was watch Benji struggle as he died in sheer agony with their eyes locked on each other. The images of that event are still vivid to Gary, like a horror stuck on replay, haunting him over and over to this day. I will continue to plead with God to somehow free him from the shackles of that recurring nightmare and bring some kind of positive purpose to his suffering.

．◆．

These are the kinds of prices we Veterans pay for the freedoms Americans are able to enjoy. All we ask is that you exercise your rights and freedoms with gratitude, respect, common sense, and dignity. Be the kind of patriots that we would not hesitate to fight for again. Please don't send our gallant men and women off to war again unless you provide us all of the support and resources necessary to win, so that our sacrifices won't feel meaningless. There also needs to be some kind of program to un-train us from all of the warrior skills and instincts we've become experts in prior to turning us loose back into civilian life.

Think about it: when you enter the military, you spend 10 weeks in Basic Training learning how to look, think, and become an obedient soldier, giving up the luxury of having your own way and thinking for yourself. You learn about and become familiar with weapons that can kill and destroy. Even your body is conditioned to become a weapon. After Basic, you spend several more months honing your respective military specialties; mine was infantry tactics. Once completed, you are then deployed to your duty assignment; mine was Vietnam. Upon arriving there, I was given two more weeks of Jungle Warfare training. Finally, after a year or more of actually fighting and surviving in a war, you are sent home. In my case, immediately after finishing my tour in Vietnam, just 72 hours fresh out of the battlefield, I was discharged from the Army, sent home, and released back into civilian life. All this happened without any "Un-training" on how *not to be a warrior anymore*, and I was expected to somehow be able to readjust back to being humane again. No one told us about the difficulties we would face transitioning back into civilian life.

Neither were we given a list of any resources to aid us with the challenges that lay ahead, not even a "Thanks for your service" or "Have a good life."

ENOUGH IS ENOUGH

The summer of 1968 marked the approaching end of my tour in Nam. It was an extremely hot, humid, and exhausting day. We were on top of Hill 352, engaged in a raging battle with a regiment of NVA Regulars attempting to assault and overtake our position. The air was filled with ear-splitting explosions and bullets crackling all around us, with screams of our wounded crying out and gurgling in pain.

I remember hearing voices screaming, "Oh God, I'm hit, I'm hit!" Others yelling, "Medic, Medic," or "No one's covering our West now, someone cover the...Ahhh, I'm hit!" While someone frantically shouted on the radio, "Fire

mission, fire mission, damn it, we need support."
All the while, one of the Dinks was blowing a
bugle signaling to charge our line, and others
hollering, "G.I. YOU DIE, G.I. YOU DIE!!!"

Some of our guys shouting back in response,
"EAT SH—T AND DIE YOU GOOK!" It was as
if I was trapped in an ear-splittingly loud echo
chamber in the middle of a tornado of all of these
sounds, heat, smoke, and smell of blood swirling
around me faster and faster.

After what seemed like a lifetime of endless
days and nights surrounded by so much carnage
and wondering who would be next while trying
not to think it might be me, I felt as though I had
had enough and finally reached my breaking point.
In war, the longer you survive, the greater the fear
that you won't, keeps whispering in the back of
your mind. I became so overwhelmed with dread
and started to breathe with rapid, shallow breaths
while trembling uncontrollably from panic. *I lost
all desire to fight and the ability to function.*

I dropped my rifle so that I could cover my
ears with my hands.

I just wanted to hide and escape from the now muffled echoes of my surroundings. In desperation, I vaguely remember abandoning my fighting position to crawl into a nearby bomb crater and covering myself up with a tarp in an effort to make this hell go away.

It was so hot and noisy, and I was overcome with profuse torrents of sweat and fear. I must have passed out because the next thing I was aware of was "Bean" pulling the tarp off of me, frantically yelling, "No, no, Tony, not you, are you hit, are you ok?" He then hollered for help to pull me out of that dirt oven and load me onto the Medivac chopper. All the while I was kicking and screaming, "Get me out of here, I want to go home. I want to go home."

I blanked out again, only to wake up later in the aid station at a base camp field hospital, with nurses cutting off all of my fatigues and jamming an IV needle in my arm while splashing ice-cold alcohol all over me in front of a large fan blowing on me in an effort to quickly lower my temperature. My medical report stated that I had suffered from heat stroke. I knew better, though. I got heat stroke because I panicked, I cracked, and put myself in that pressure-cooker oven under that suffocating tarp. I felt like such a failure, like such a wimp, like such a shameful coward who abandoned his comrades in the heat of battle and let them down.

After a few days in recovery, I was ordered back to the field, but I tried to think of ways to avoid going back out to my unit so that I wouldn't have to face my guys. I felt so ashamed. Once again, I took a deep breath and said to myself...... "IT DON'T MEAN NUTHIN, NOT A DAMN THANG," but deep down inside it did, and it still does to this day.

I may not have been wounded physically, but I still carry those shameful scars of survivor's guilt. To my relief, I was sent to sub in another platoon that was shorthanded on squad leaders. I finished out the rest of my tour there while avoiding any opportunity to inquire about the fate of my remaining friends from the original Fort Hood 3rd Platoon.... more sandbags added to my heart's emotional fortress.

⚜

Out of the 42 original people in the 3rd Platoon who started off with me from Fort Hood, Texas, only 3 or 4 of us survived without being killed or wounded. Gary got a Purple Heart for his wounds, and Bean got 3 Purple Hearts for the times he was wounded. Benji was awarded the Silver Star posthumously. For many years, whenever Gary, Bean, and I would gather for our annual post-war reunion, I have felt ironically unworthy to be in their company because I didn't pay nearly the same price that they did by not once shedding any of my own blood. Once again, survivor's guilt.... more sandbags added to my heart's now impenetrable protective fortress.

I did, however, on far too many occasions, come within inches of getting my name on the Vietnam Memorial Wall. Once, after a fierce firefight, I pointed out to Gary that he had a pretty nasty bullet crease in his helmet, to which he laughed out loud and pointed out a bullet hole through my shirt just under my left armpit. Eight more inches to the right, and it would have been lights out, and my name would have been forever etched on "The Wall." I also keep a replica of one of the ammo pouches that I wore in front of my right hip, with 2 AK-47 bullet holes through it. In country, I used to carry a small California flag with me that I would often plant in the ground in front of my foxhole. It also had a few bullet holes in it. Needless to say, it didn't take me long to discontinue that "bullet magnet" practice.

-♦-

I desperately wanted to put the pain of losing friends and the memories of the gruesome things I had witnessed behind me, but "Out of sight and out of mind" was an impossible challenge.

-♦-

The thing about sandbags is that when dried after being wet, they become as hard as cement. I secretly shed tears over each added sandbag. Little did I realize that the barricade around my heart became so impenetrable that it ultimately changed from being my sanctuary to becoming my prison... no one in and nothing out.

.♦.

After what felt like an eternity spent in hell, my tour of duty was finally up, and orders to catch the next chopper out of the boonies came through. I gathered up all my gear and distributed my remaining ammo, grenades, and C-rations to my comrades who I was leaving behind. One by one, I wished them well, making unkept promises to visit and say " Hello" to their parents. I was given the honor to pop the smoke grenade to guide the incoming supply helicopter in to pick me up and initiate my exit out of Nam and out of the Army. One memento that I still have today is the pull-ring from that smoke grenade. Now I wear it on a chain around my neck, reminding me that the last grenade I ever threw was not to kill, but to guide in my chariot ride out of that brutal nightmare. It now represents that I made it-*I survived.*

Those days are over, and are now more than 20,000 plus days and some 9,000 miles behind me.

BACK IN
THE WORLD

NO LONGER A SOLDIER

You would think that after every waking hour for the past year, the fear of getting killed and not ever seeing home again always lurking in the back of my mind, that finally jumping on an airliner on my final leg of heading home would be my top priority. Oddly, though, I didn't quite feel ready. I felt dirty and afraid that the things I've done and experienced would be a potential for rejection by my friends and family. After being released from the military in Fort Lewis, Washington, I opted instead to spend a couple of days in Portland, Oregon, with my buddy Larry from Nam, who got out a month prior to me. We shared many drinks while reminiscing over our shared war experiences. He warned me of the social aversion to the war and its participants and how to *not* let it get the best of me "Cuz it don't mean nuthin," just be thankful that we got out vertically. After a couple of days, I felt ready to face my parents and boarded an airplane heading to San Francisco.

Landing there, I was shocked at my first sight of hippies. No neat razor-cut hairdos, button-down collars, white Levis, and Converse tennis shoes like before I left. Now I saw people with long, dirty hair, long sideburns with big mustaches, pastel-colored sunglasses, and bell-bottom pants. Wow, did I feel out of place being well-groomed with shined shoes in my dress green uniform adorned with insignias, ribbons, and medals indicating that I served and fought well. I walked past one such hippie-looking guy who actually sneered at me, spat at me, and called me a coward for not refusing to go to Vietnam. The pride of wearing that uniform, indicating that I faithfully served my country, started to fade into puzzling shame.

-♦-

My parents didn't know that I was on my way home yet. My plan was to hop on a commuter helicopter at San Francisco Airport, fly across the bay to Oakland Airport, then catch a taxi home to San Leandro, about 10 miles away, to surprise my family. I got my ticket for the helicopter, but fifteen minutes before the scheduled flight, my name was called to the check-in counter. There, I was informed that my seat had been bumped because civilians were given priority seating over military standby personnel. I figured, No problem. I've waited a year to get home; I can wait a little longer. The next available flight would be in about thirty minutes, so I complied.

A few minutes before that next flight, the same thing happened. Again, I was being bumped off for someone else. I tried to explain that I was actually now a civilian, but the uniform I was wearing was the only clothes I had. I even showed the ticket agent my discharge papers and told her that I had been overseas, and all I wanted was to get home and see my family, who had been worried about me for the last twelve months. She apologized and promised to get me on the next flight after the lunch hour. Angrily, I slammed my ticket on the counter and demanded a refund while she muttered something under her breath about me being a crazy, wild animal. Now that my plan had been ruined, I found a payphone and called my parents to tell them where I was so that they could come get me.

Once home, and after all of the excitement and tears of joy subsided, still in uniform, I borrowed my dad's car and drove over to the house of the girl I went steady with prior to going overseas. (For privacy reasons, I'll refer to her as "Jane.") I was so anxious to see the girl who kept me fighting to survive for the past twelve long months. Jane's mother greeted me at the door but awkwardly invited me in. I sat in her living room and was told that Jane was out shopping but should return soon.

Soon, Jane's younger brother excitedly bolted into the room, exclaiming, "Hey, guess what? I'm going to be an uncle!" His mother tried to hush him up and finally somberly said, "I'm so very sorry, but Jane got herself into trouble while you were gone." Not really wanting confirmation, I asked what she meant, and she ashamedly informed me, "It was a big mess, but now she is pregnant." Stunned and bewildered, at a total loss for words, I excused myself and just left. I got in the car dazed, heartbroken, and full of rage. I stomped on the gas pedal and screeched away, leaving two long black lines on the pavement, evidence of my anger, hurt, and rage.

The only thing I wanted to do was head straight for the local recruiting office to reenlist and request to be shipped back to Vietnam. I believed that at least back in Nam, I had some black-and-white control over my day-to-day existence, where it would be acceptable to violently vent my rage and hatred. Coming to a screeching stop in front of the recruiter's office, I encountered yet another obstacle to my happy homecoming expectations. The recruiting office was closed because it just happened to be Sunday. I screamed a blistering "WELCOME *&$@*^#@ HOME @$%&(*^$!!!

⚜

I have since realized how grateful I should be to God that He didn't allow me to go back to

Vietnam. I had a cousin who had the exact same kind of devastating news about returning home to a pregnant girlfriend and re-enlisted to go back to Nam. Tragically, he ended up getting his name on the Vietnam Memorial Wall in Washington, D.C.

-♦-

I remember sitting at the dinner table with my parents and brother on that first night home, and I accidentally dropped some food on the floor. My knee-jerk reaction was to just blurt out an "F-BOMB" then trying to cover it up with the "SH-BOMB" followed by taking the Lord's name in vain, ending in leaving the table with an "F-ing" apology. My mother's tear-filled eyes bulged with shock. With that, my Dad, who served in the Navy during WWII, tried to console my bewildered mother by explaining that's just how you talk in the military.

Thus began my desperate quest to recapture the happy-go-lucky, trusting, naïve, fun-loving guy that I once was. I had no idea that trying to figure out who and how I was now supposed to be turned into a decades-long excavation project.

I knew how to walk point, set up an ambush, tell where shots came from, set booby traps, get rid of leeches, throw a grenade, dress a head wound, apply a tourniquet, call in an artillery strike, and shoot people. I had become *really* good at the skills needed to fight and survive, but now had to relearn things that were no longer second nature to me, like being "civilized." Things like how to talk without cuss words, how to relax, and not be on constant alert. Even seemingly silly, insignificant things like remembering I can now use and flush a toilet, change into clean clothes daily, shower as often as I want, not eat so hurriedly, remember to say please and thank you, and even get to eat whatever, sound appetizing to me.

Having to explain to the people that the reason for my difficulties in readjusting to civilization was because of the war, embittered me. Sadly, being a participant in that war was not looked upon as an honorable or patriotic way to serve our country. The pride I felt from bravely serving my country quickly deteriorated into contradictory shame. The lack of closure from not being allowed to win what I believed was definitely a winnable war intensified my questioning of why God let good people die horrific deaths, and for what purpose, what did it accomplish? And why should I be made to feel ashamed for doing what so many others are not brave enough to do?

I felt the need to just wear a happy face and lie, saying that I had been stationed in Germany. Instead of maintaining a well-groomed military appearance, I let my hair grow long and donned ragged hippy-style clothing in an effort to blend in and not to be identified as "One of those cowards who refused to participate in the Vietnam War." It also seems ironic that back then, we were labeled as "Baby Killers" in light of today's controversy over abortion rights.

-◆-

Looking back, I've had several jobs and relationships that I took for granted. I now see that I hurt many people with my inability to let anyone in too close to my heart. Whenever I realized that I was starting to care "too much" about someone or something, I would invent some kind of discontentment with them and move on. I became good at deflecting my faults and insecurities onto others so that I wouldn't have to place the blame on the real me. During the war, I had to learn how not to allow myself to feel too close to anyone because it always hurt too deeply to lose them. That was the problem with the mantra "It don't mean nuthin."

That mantra is the most tragic double negative truth of combat.

Out of necessity, I learned it so well that I didn't realize I needed to unlearn it. Unfortunately, others around me had to suffer the consequences, and for that I am so deeply sorry.

I especially want to apologize to my daughters for being emotionally absent during their key developmental years while I was searching for that elusive "normal" man that I thought I was supposed to be. I'm embarrassed to admit that I often fell far short of being a reliable friend, husband, and father.

All around me, life was like a festival of activity. I desperately wanted to join in, but my conditioning to be constantly cautious prevented me from letting my guard down. I had become conditioned into believing that any joy, fun, or meaningful relationship was just a fleeting prelude to eventual mayhem, disappointment, and tragedy.

My ability to care about others to any depth or intimacy was blocked by my now unnecessary, excessive need for emotional preservation. It caused me to be quick to judge, criticize, and form assumptions about others based on my own biases, misperceptions, or unvetted hearsay. My stunted emotions and selfish desires were not the most reliable guides for my decisions.

In an effort to fit in, I created a façade of friendly charm, good nature, and quick humor to cloak my repressed discontentment, restlessness, and brokenness. Emotional numbness concealed the true condition of my impenetrable heart. I became unable to function freely, handicapped and hindered from willingly engaging with "friendlies" to my full potential, always holding back what I believed was the most vulnerable part of me. I was so self-absorbed with my own "better idea," or "more significant" point, or more "interesting" experiences that I would often rudely interrupt or speak over other people's conversations. I refused to recognize that I was often rude, distant, unaffectionate, or insensitive to those around me. The thought never crossed my mind to think, look, or interact outside of my calcified self.

I'm not making excuses or looking to justify my insensitive blunders. Nor am I seeking sympathy. I simply want to acknowledge them and now sincerely apologize to everyone I've hurt or offended, so that they can be assured that it was never anything they did wrong or how they may have mistreated me. I've always viewed you all as people of high character; otherwise, I would not have been drawn to you. It was I who was not behaving in a way worthy of your friendship, trust, or love. It was I who didn't have a malleable heart.

We, Veterans, didn't choose to be that way, but unfortunately, many choose to stay that way or seek unhealthy ways to self-medicate, hoping that time will heal their wounds. It won't; time only helps you get used to the pain and unhealthy emotional state. Talking about and admitting our hurts, fears, and faults takes far more courage and strength than it does to keep it stuffed down inside, but the freedom from opening up about them is exceedingly more rewarding.

You can't change your past, you can only choose to find a different perspective about it and share that wisdom to encourage others. We all have the choice to either dwell in the past and accept it as a life sentence or know that there is hope to be able to make peace with your demons.

In Nam, we didn't dare "jinx" our future by looking forward to or planning on an existence beyond just the here and now. Tomorrow, next week, or next year seemed far too fragile to believe in. That mindset is no longer valid or necessary. True, none of us are guaranteed tomorrow, but why waste today worrying over what we can't prevent and miss out on the fruits of what can be today?

MY TRANSFORMATION

John 16:33 (NIV)

"I have told you these things so that in Me you may have peace. In this world you will have trouble, but take heart! I have overcome the world!"

A life void of challenges is not promised anywhere in the Bible, but they don't have to be your master. We are promised that with God, I don't have to face them alone, figure out my own solutions, or be overwhelmed by them.

My experiences from 1967 and 1968 caused me to believe that God was unfair, unjust, and apathetic. I began to believe that God was a liar, that God was a lie, so much so that I had no interest in ever going to church or acknowledging my need for His existence. Looking back, I now can see that even though I abandoned Him, He *never abandoned me.*

Psalm 139:8 (NKJV)

Where can I go from Your Spirit? Or where can I flee from Your presence? If I ascend into Heaven, You are there; If I make my bed in hell, behold, You are there.

In light of my numerous close calls, and even when I had to sleep waist-deep in filthy rice paddy water, He was there in Vietnam. God's plans for who He created me to become were far more resilient than that sandbag fortification that I built around my heart.

.&.

In 1979, God's blessings started to become evident in my life. I was working for a local potato chip company as a delivery driver. In the afternoon, after completing our delivery routes, we would return to the warehouse to restock our delivery trucks for the next day's deliveries. While in the warehouse gathering boxes of product, I heard a woman's laughter coming from the next aisle. I was so intrigued by that delightfully angelic sound that I just had to find out who it belonged to. Rounding the corner of that aisle, I caught my first glimpse of "HER." She was standing there giggling and talking with a few other co-workers. She looked so charming and delightfully beautiful. I thought to myself, "Forget it dummy, she's way out of your league." To my surprise, she turned to me, sweetly smiled, extended her hand to shake mine, and said, "Hi, I'm Debbie." Wow, I thought I had just been touched by an angel. Little did I realize that I was looking into the eyes of one of God's most precious lifelong blessings for me.

Somehow, to my extreme delight, we became a couple and were married in 1981. Debbie had a daughter, Jennifer, from a previous marriage, who was 3 years old when we met. I also had two daughters, Kimiya, 8, and Katrina, 5, from a previous marriage, and they would stay with us every other weekend. Life was great, but shortly afterwards, I started becoming an overly demanding stepfather to Jennifer. I felt that since I couldn't be around my own two daughters 24/7, Jennifer was not going to receive more attention and affection from me than my two girls. The irony, however, was that I wasn't even very attentive or affectionate to Kimiya and Katrina. It was evidence, though, that sandbags still remained that needed to be dismantled from around my heart.

-♦-

Debbie and I seldom argued about anything except for my ill treatment towards Jennifer. Debbie was always supportive and sympathetic to my struggles with nightmares and flashbacks, and by the grace of God, chose not to give up on me. Debbie was raised attending a Church of Christ, but because of their seemingly strict rules and teachings of condemnation, she never felt particularly passionate about religion or going to church. However, she did want to give Jennifer an opportunity to have some exposure to know about God. Debbie decided to have Jennifer start attending a Baptist elementary school. One day,

Jennifer came from school exuberantly exclaiming, "Mom, Mom, I got saved today, I got saved today!"

In a momma bear panic, Debbie fired back, "Saved from what!? What happened? Was anybody hurt? Are you OK?" Jennifer happily replied that she accepted Jesus into her heart. In her innocent, childlike five-year-old way, she tried to explain what that meant. Debbie didn't fully understand, but not wanting to dampen Jennifer's joy, she simply said, "Good for you, honey, I'm really happy for you."

Later, Debbie asked me if I knew what all that meant. I shrugged my shoulders and could only say, "Huh, I've never heard of that sort of thing." A few weeks later, Jennifer started questioning why we didn't go to church. Our vague reply was always, "Maybe someday."

One of Debbie's sisters, Sheryl, who also grew up in the same strict Church of Christ environment, told her she had started going to a church that was very different than what they had ever experienced. It was a church that taught that God was not a figure who got mad or was always looking for reasons to punish and condemn us to hell. But rather a kind, loving, and compassionate God who deeply longed for an intimate relationship with us, not wanting us to struggle through life on our own, but wants to do life *with us*. She also said that they even had live music, which she'd never experienced before, and that was very uplifting, encouraging, and joyful.

It only took Sheryl a couple of invitations to get Debbie to join her before Debbie decided to go. Debbie came home one Sunday after attending for the first time with a joyful smile. She told me that it was so very different from any other church service she had ever attended and that she really liked it. She tried to encourage me to give it a try, but I said, "That's nice, Babe, but I'm good. You go if it makes you happy."

Debbie started attending regularly and brought Jennifer to the children's ministry service. After a month or so, I started noticing a difference in both of them. They seemed to have a different sense of contentment. Sometimes, I would catch

Debbie quietly humming or singing "church" songs. I don't remember exactly how long it took, but eventually, curiosity got the best of me, and *I had to check this church thing out.* The protective side of me wanted to make sure that they weren't being scammed by some kind of cult.

So there I sat in church for the first time in a very, very long time, arms tightly crossed, convinced that I wasn't going to be impressed. I looked around at all of the people exchanging pleasantries, thinking what a bunch of silly pretenders they all must be. I'll bet none of them could have possibly been where I've been. Then, the worship music started, and I started to feel strangely choked up. I couldn't understand why I was starting to weep.

I was confused and tried my best to clear my throat and secretly hide my attempts to wipe away traces of my tears. In my mind, I justified my emotional state on too much alcohol from the night before.

At that time, I was a lounge lizard frequently performing in bars and dinner houses. After closing for the night, the workers and I would often gather around the bar for a little "Partying." Back in church, I convinced myself that my nervous system was probably just fragile from being hungover. It sounded like a logical explanation for my weepy state. I reasoned that I should try church again next Sunday, but maybe leave out alcohol the night before just to see if the same thing would happen. The following weekend, I didn't party on Saturday night, but the same thing happened in church the next morning. I started paying attention to what the Pastor was teaching and heard a few things that captured my attention.

I'm not judging or criticizing Catholicism, and maybe it's different now, but growing up Catholic, I don't recall ever being instructed or encouraged to read the Holy Bible. I don't even remember seeing any evidence of a bible being present in any of my fellow Catholic friends' or relatives' homes. There was no need to research scripture. We just obeyed what we were told and taught by the priests and nuns without question, and in doing so, we would be good to go with God. In this new church that I started attending, we were encouraged and even instructed to read and study all of the scriptures in the Bible, which are the very words from God Himself given to us through His prophets and disciples.

Wow, I never considered that it could be possible for any of us to interact directly with God Almighty Himself instead of having to go through a priest or Mary. I never knew that the curtain that separated all of the people from the entering into the Holiest of Holy part of the temple, where God was said to dwell, was torn open the moment of Jesus' death, symbolizing that we, as followers of Christ, are no longer prevented from fully entering into the very throne room of God! Or that I no longer have to go to a priest to confess and be forgiven for my sins, and that I can simply go *directly to God in prayer* for forgiveness without having to recite repetitive, unaffectionate, and insincere scripted prayers. Why is it that no one ever told me these things?

Matthew 27:50-51 (NIV)

And when Jesus had cried out again in a loud voice, He gave up His spirit.

At that moment, the curtain of the temple was torn in two from top to bottom. The earth shook, the rocks split...

The more I discovered who God really is, the more I recognized my need to unlearn my distrust in Him. My transformation into a "normal" person was not immediate or dramatic. In fact, it took decades for me to become that elusive "Tony" that I so desperately wanted to feel contented and comfortable with being.

There have been many ups and downs, highs and lows, victories and failures, but as God's Word promises, I didn't and never will have to go through any of it alone ever again.

John 16:33 (NIV)

"I have told you these things, so that in Me you may have peace. In this world you will have trouble. But take heart! I have overcome the world."

Deuteronomy 31:8 (AMP)

It is the Lord who goes before you; He will be with you. He will not fail you or abandon you. Do not fear or be dismayed."

I still may take three steps forward and two steps back, but at least I keep moving in a positive direction now. It's as though God is gradually, tenderly, and lovingly removing the sandbags of my emotional bunker. He may remove three sandbags, and I'll put back two, but at least I am moving closer and closer, little by little, to that malleable-hearted man He created me to be.

One thing that worked for me was learning to shift my focus off of myself by being of service to others. I have learned that one of the callings in Christianity is becoming an influencer of comfort, encouragement, and compassion. God guided me to volunteer at a local VA Hospital, helping in the homeless department or pushing Veterans in wheelchairs to and from appointments. The VA also had a program called "No Veteran Dies Alone." Whenever a patient in the hospital was terminally ill but had no friends or relatives able to be with them in their last hours of life, we would stay by their bedside for a few hours just to talk, read, or pray with them until they passed.

Unfortunately, the Chaplain who piloted that program retired, and there was no one available to take over leading it. Serving in these programs gave me a brief opportunity to chat with the Vets, hear their stories, and learn about the health or life issues that they struggled with. It helped me to appreciate that either my problems weren't so different, or maybe not as devastating as theirs.

One time, I got called to pick up a patient who needed to be wheeled to the Oncology Department. Upon arriving at the reception area, I discovered that the patient was a dear friend of mine, Rick, who was there for chemotherapy treatment for pancreatic cancer. It was quite a delight to see him, but awfully concerning to learn of his ailment. Still, it was an honor to have been there to encourage and pray over him while wheeling him to and from his appointments. I thank God that I can now report that Rick is in complete remission and doing well again.

Another organization that I was able to volunteer with was called "CERT" (Community Emergency Response Team). There, I obtained certification in CPR, Critical Bleeding Control, Search and Rescue techniques, and first-line injury triage. We assisted the police department with missing-person searches and traffic control, and the fire department with cooling stations, energy snacks, and Gatorade, during lengthy fire calls. Additionally, we managed First Aid stations at the Community Festival events. Service to others really helped realign my focus, pulling me out of my own bubble and onto those in need of help or encouragement.

At one point, I participated in a Veteran's Support group consisting of combat vets from Desert Storm, Afghanistan, Iraq, but only one other person who served in Vietnam. When I joined the meeting, I mentioned how I resented those Middle East Vets for the welcome home and accolades they received that we never did.

However, after hearing their stories and struggles with triggers that caused their flashbacks and nightmares, I recognized that their issues were no different from mine. By the end of our 12-week session, I felt compelled to tell them that I no longer resented them, just envied them, and stood up and saluted them all. In return, they all thanked us Vietnam Vets for fighting for the resources they now benefit from.

It's amusing to me how often, during support groups or PTSD psych evaluations for VA disability benefits, the question of whether or not I've ever considered harming myself or taking my own life always comes up. Shockingly, to them, my honest answer is always, "Yes. But, I definitely would not! Because to do so would mean that the Viet Cong finally got me, and I refuse to give him that victory."

-♦-

Church is a subject I once considered to be a turn-off, and you might be feeling the same right now, but this is what has worked for me. My hope and prayer is that one day, you would be open-minded enough to consider my example. As I mentioned before, I grew up with a religion that never encouraged reading the Bible; in fact, it even promoted beliefs that weren't exactly biblical. The nondenominational church that I started attending was very different. First of all, I learned that in:

2 Timothy 3:16 (NIV)

All Scripture is God-breathed and is useful for teaching, rebuking, correcting and training in righteousness.

Also, the end of the bible warns:

Revelation 22:18-19 (NIV)

I warn everyone who hears the words of the prophecy of this scroll: If anyone adds anything to them, God will add to that person the plagues described in this scroll. And if anyone takes words away from this scroll of prophecy, God will take away from that person any share in the tree of Life and in the Holy City, which are described in this scroll.

These scriptures grabbed my attention, increasing my curiosity of misconceptions I had about my Creator.

Having played solo guitar and sung in lounges and restaurants, I thought it gave me enough skills to join the worship team. Once I had gotten past the mindset of "Check me out, I can play guitar and sing," and began paying attention to the lyrics of the newly discovered contemporary Christian songs I was singing, my heart started to become more saturated with the love, hope, truth, faith, and forgiveness that I was singing about.

Learning and memorizing Biblical principles in this way is similar to how we all learned the alphabet as kids. Remember how we would sing the A-B-C song? For the first time, I wasn't doing music to entertain or impress people; first and foremost, I was thanking and praising God for all the answered prayers, provisions, and protections He blesses me with. Additionally, serving in a way that helps the congregation connect in a more intimate way with God.

I also started connecting and fellowshipping with groups of people who spoke hope, truth, love, and encouragement into me. Praying together and for each other was also a new experience. It's more than just another way of serving others. It is an enormous honor and blessing to be a contributor of encouragement, comfort, and a positive influencer for a change rather than a needy consumer.

I said at the beginning of this book, you can take the soldier out of the war, but you can't take the war out of the soldier. While that is true, I still carry those memories and images in my mind, but they are only *in my mind* and **no longer in my heart.** They no longer disturb me or have the ability to diminish the depth of my peace, joy, contentment, or love. A very dear friend and spiritual mentor of mine, Paul Rider, calls it "Heart Peace." He has shared a multitude of Biblical truths and spiritual pearls of wisdom with me. Things like:

James 1:5 (NIV)

If any of you lacks wisdom, you should ask God, who gives generously to all without finding fault, and it will be given to you.

Paul encouraged me to simply ask God for spiritual wisdom every day and see what happens. So I began, and suddenly found myself on a fast path to more spiritual growth than ever before.

"SIT REP" (SITUATION REPORT)

I am definitely still a work in progress, but the sandbags are gone, and now I'm okay with the man I see in the mirror. I now see evidence of God's fingerprints all over my life. He's been guiding me, shaping me, and cleaning off my barnacles of unbelief and mistrust. My heart still bears the scars, but they are only remnants of wounds that are now healed.

As I mentioned earlier, they are no longer painful and inflamed. They no longer dictate my mood, joy, and peace. Do I still have flashbacks? Yes, but my flashbacks only remind me, with gratitude, of God's mercy, grace, and healing love. Am I still hypervigilant? Yes, but my focus has shifted to being watchful for opportunities to thank God for His goodness and blessings, and for ways to bless, comfort, and encourage others. Do I still have challenging times in my life? Absolutely, but now I no longer have to confront them alone. It's far more "energy-saving" to see them as opportunities to learn and grow stronger.

I have repeatedly discovered that the gospel of Jesus Christ is much bigger than *anything I could ever struggle with*. I am discovering "Heart peace." *None of this* is "religion." I have tried religion and only found it to be an impossible task to keep a checklist of dos and don'ts that always left me feeling like a condemned, frustrated failure headed for hell. What I have discovered and live by daily is a personal, intimate *relationship* with God through Jesus Christ. It's not that He loves me more than anyone else, He just listens and takes care of me because **I have invited Him into my life**.

One other thing that many of us have struggled with is, "Why does God allow bad and often tragic things to happen to good people?" Our human minds are not capable of understanding the mind, reasons, or plans of God, but this I do know and believe. For one thing, the Bible says:

Isaiah 55:8-9 (NIV)

For My thoughts are not your thoughts, neither are your ways My ways, declares the Lord. As the heavens are higher than the earth, so are My ways higher than your ways and My thoughts than your thoughts.

Because of Adam and Eve, we are all born into a world of imperfections in life, justice, unity, humanity, love, morality, and more. God created our world with perfection. Just look at the majesty and beauty of our mountains, oceans, sunsets, and perfectly synchronized seasons. Humans are the ones who corrupted this harmoniously intended place with greed, lust, hatred, and selfish desires. God does not cause bad things to happen and certainly did not create our world to include them. He uses our hardship to cause us to long for a more permanent place of peace and perfection. Unfortunately for all of us, that place only exists in Heaven. Zach Gryder, one of the pastors at my church, stated so profoundly, "Not all suffering comes with purpose, but all suffering can be *given purpose* when placed in the hands of God."

You may be someone who likes to think of yourself as deserving Heaven just because "I'm a reasonably good person." But reasonably good isn't quite good enough.

John 14:6 (NIV)

Jesus answered, "I am the way and the truth and the life. No one comes to the Father except through Me.

Romans 10:9 (NIV)

If you declare with your mouth, "Jesus is Lord," and believe in your heart that God raised Him from the dead, you will be saved.

All you have to do is say and *believe* those two verses and *invite* Jesus into your heart to be your Lord and Savior, and your eternity in Heaven is locked in with no uncertainties.

Christ's resurrection from death reassures me that no situation, mistake, or offence is beyond God's power or willingness to redeem. There is no fear Jesus cannot overcome, no life He can't revive.

My personal relationship of a life with Christ isn't a crutch; it has been my life raft. All of my disappointments, flaws, and failings only confirm my need to draw closer to Jesus with deep gratitude and relief, reminding me that there is not, nor ever will be, any condemnation or rejection for those who choose to accept Jesus Christ as their Lord and Savior.

Acts 20:24 (NIV)

However, I consider my life worth nothing to me; my only aim is to finish the race and complete the task the Lord Jesus has given me — the task of testifying to the good news of God's grace.

We are all given a finite number of chapters in our life story. It can either be one that glorifies God by encouraging, loving, or comforting others, or one that does not. The choice is ours to make. We are all given a finite number of chapters in our life story. It can either be one that glorifies God by encouraging, loving, or comforting others, or one that does not. The choice is ours to make. After inviting Him into your heart, sit with Him to build a relationship. Ask Him to show you that He does exist. He wants to show you that He is good, not once in a while, but all of the time. If you want to hear Him, take time to listen.

> *"Be still, and know that I am God."*
>
> **Psalm 46:10 (NIV)**

"The Dash" is a famous poem by Linda Ellis that basically says that on everyone's tombstone, the dates are etched. Between those two dates is a dash. What matters most is that "Dash." It represents how you lived and what you did during your time here on Earth. Everyone's dash is their legacy-what kind of influencer were you, positive or negative? Even though my dash may have started off looking more like an EKG graph, my confidence is now on an upswing, pointing towards Heaven. For such a long wasted time, I was living without any forward, backward, left or right, up or down. It was like I was just stuck in neutral. But it was as if God got my heart truly beating again and breathed life back into a non-compassionate, non-trusting, unable-to-love-deeply narcissistic heart.

If you have been searching and longing for "Heart Peace," please let me know: tfunt1968@gmail.com. It would be my joy and honor to pray for you. Or find a church that is Bible based and teaches about and promotes God, our loving Father and Creator, Jesus, our Lord and Savior, and the Holy Spirit, our Counselor and Comforter, in equal amounts of deity.

My prayer for you all comes from:

Numbers 6:24-26 (NIV)

The Lord bless you and keep you;
the Lord make His face shine on you
and be gracious to you;
the Lord turn His face toward you
and give you peace."

REFLECTION

These are just a few of the many promises of God that are found in the Bible. Now that I've invited Jesus Christ to be my Lord and Savior, my life is a living testament that God never has broken and never will break any of His promises.

2 Corinthians 5:17 (ESV)

Therefore, if anyone is in Christ, he is a new creation. The old has passed away; behold, the new has come.

Ephesians 4:22-24 (ESV)

To put off your old self, which belongs to your former manner of life and is corrupt through deceitful desires, and to be renewed in the spirit of your minds, and to put on the new self, created after the likeness of God in true righteousness and holiness.

Ezekiel 36:26

"I will remove the heart of stone from your flesh and give you a heart of flesh."

2 Corinthians 3:18

Our justification is instantaneous, but our sanctification is a process, so press toward the mark and be patient with yourself. He is taking us from one degree of glory to the next.

Proverbs 3:5-6 (ESV)

Trust in the Lord with all your heart, and do not lean on your own understanding. In all your ways acknowledge Him, and He will make straight your paths.

Romans 10:9-10 (ESV)

...because, if you confess with your mouth that Jesus is Lord and believe in your heart that God raised Him from the dead, you will be saved. For with the heart one believes and is justified, and with the mouth one confesses and is saved.

Philippians 4:7 (NIV)

And the peace of God, which transcends all understanding, will guard your hearts and your minds in Christ Jesus.

Psalms 23:4 (NASB)

Even though I walk through the valley of the shadow of death, I fear no evil, for You are with me;

Even though I've walked through the A Shau Valley shadow of death, I will fear no evil. For You were there with me in Vietnam, even though I didn't know it.

(Paraphrasing from the song "Amazing Grace," a Christian hymn written in 1772 and published in 1779 by English Anglican clergyman and poet John Newton)

I was lost, now found, blind but now I see, finally becoming the man I was created to be.

ABOUT THE AUTHOR

 Tony is originally from California and is now retired, living in Texas. He is blessed with his wonderful wife, Debbie; three amazing daughters; he is a grandfather to five wonderful young women and four fantastic young men; and a great-grandson.

He served in the U.S. Army from 1966 to 1968. The last year was spent fighting in Vietnam as a Sergeant E-5 Infantry Squad Leader of the 3rd Platoon, Charlie Company, with the 198th Light Infantry Brigade of the Americal Division. He is also the recipient of the Bronze Star.

For the past 20 years, Tony has been involved with church worship teams as a rhythm guitar player and vocalist. He has written several contemporary Christian worship songs and is also the author of *Parables From Combat: Scriptures Through the Eyes of a Combat Veteran*.

Despite his traumatic war experiences, Tony can now reflect and see how God was with him throughout. He recognizes how God took all his pain, suffering, and struggles to find true peace and added purpose by using his testimony to help others find similar healing. All of this is done with deep gratitude and all the glory to God.

To connect with Tony, email TFunt1968@gmail.com.